SILVER·BURDETT

Making Music

Program Authors

Jane Beethoven
Susan Brumfield
Patricia Shehan Campbell
David N. Connors
Robert A. Duke
Judith A. Jellison

Rita Klinger
Rochelle Mann
Hunter C. March
Nan L. McDonald
Marvelene C. Moore
Mary Palmer
Konnie Saliba

Will Schmid
Carol Scott-Kassner
Mary E. Shamrock
Sandra L. Stauffer
Judith Thomas
Jill Trinka

PEARSON
Scott Foresman

Editorial Offices: Glenview, Illinois • Parsippany, New Jersey • New York, New York
Sales Offices: Needham, Massachusetts • Duluth, Georgia • Glenview, Illinois
Coppell, Texas • Sacramento, California • Mesa, Arizona

ISBN: 0-382-36570-4
2008 Edition
Copyright © 2005, Pearson Education, Inc.

Contributing Authors

Audrey A. Berger
Roslyn Burrough
J. Bryan Burton
Jeffrey E. Bush
John M. Cooksey
Shelly C. Cooper
Alice-Ann Darrow
Scott Emmons
Debra Erck
Anne M. Fennell
Doug Fisher
Carroll Gonzo
Larry Harms
Martha F. Hilley
Debbie Burgoon Hines

Mary Ellen Junda
Donald Kalbach
Shirley Lacroix
Henry Leck
Sanna Longden
Glenn A. Richter
Carlos Xavier Rodriguez
Kathleen Donahue Sanz
Julie K. Scott
Gwen Spell
Barb Stevanson
Kimberly C. Walls
Jackie Wiggins
Maribeth Yoder-White

Listening Map Contributing Authors

Patricia Shehan Campbell
Jackie Chooi-Theng Lew
Ann Clements
Kay Edwards
Sheila Feay-Shaw
Kay Greenhaw

David Hebert
Hunter C. March
Carol Scott-Kassner
Mary E. Shamrock
Sandra L. Stauffer

Movement Contributing Authors

Judy Lasko
Marvelene C. Moore
Dixie Piver

Wendy Taucher
Susan Thomasson
Judith Thompson-Barthwell

Recording Producers
Buryl Red, Executive Producer

Rick Baitz
Rick Bassett
Bill and Charlene James
Joseph Joubert
Bryan Louiselle
Tom Moore
J. Douglas Pummill

Michael Rafter
Mick Rossi
Buddy Skipper
Robert Spivak
Jeanine Tesori
Linda Twine

Contents
Steps to Making Music

Unit 1 — Let the Music Begin!   2

Unit Introduction

Element	Lesson	
EXPRESSION	**1** Loud and Soft Sounds = Dynamics!	6
RHYTHM	**2** The Beat Goes On	8
	M*U*S*I*C M*A*K*E*R*S Tap Dogs	
RHYTHM	**3** Get the Rhythm	12
RHYTHM	**4** Rhythms at Rest	14
RHYTHM	**5** Rhythm Fun!	16
	Show What You Know!	
FORM	**6** Let the Spirit Move You	18
	Movement: "Michael, Row the Boat Ashore"	
MELODY	**7** Up and Down the Music Trail	20
	M*U*S*I*C M*A*K*E*R*S Aaron Copland	
	Listening Map: Buckaroo Holiday	
MELODY	**8** Follow the Direction of the Music	24
MELODY	**9** Three Pitches	26
MELODY	**10** Read Pizza, Play Pizza	28
	Arts Connection Children Playing London Bridge	
	Movement: "Pizza, Pizza, Daddy-o"	
	Show What You Know!	
TIMBRE	**11** You Are the Music	32
TEXTURE/HARMONY	**12** Thin to Thick	34
REVIEW AND ASSESS	Review, Assess, Perform, Create	36

 = Core Lesson
 = Music Reading Lesson

Unit 2 Exploring Music 38

Unit Introduction

Element	Lesson	
EXPRESSION	**1** Speed Up, Slow Down	42
	Movement: "Miss Mary Mack"	
	Arts **Connection** *Untitled*	
RHYTHM	**2** Frog Rhythms	44
RHYTHM	**3** Pick a Pattern	46
	Arts **Connection** *Rhythmical*	
	Show What You Know!	
RHYTHM	**4** Get on the Beat	50
FORM	**5** Singin' the Blues	52
	M★U★S★I★C M★A★K★E★R★S Huddie Ledbetter	
MELODY	**6** Singing Ecuador	54
	Movement: *"El juego chirimbolo"*	
MELODY	**7** Find a New Pitch	56
	Poem: "Wind Has Shaken Autumn Down"	
MELODY	**8** Name the New Pitch	58
	Show What You Know!	
MELODY	**9** Melodic Pathways	60
	Listening Map: *Shenandoah*	
TIMBRE	**10** Percussion Timbres	64
	Poem: "De Beat"	
TEXTURE/HARMONY	**11** Speaking in Layers	68
	M★U★S★I★C M★A★K★E★R★S Babatunde Olatunji	
TEXTURE/HARMONY	**12** Play a Musical Message	70
	Story: "Ayelivi"	
REVIEW AND ASSESS	Review, Assess, Perform, Create	72

Core Lesson = ⭐
Music Reading Lesson = 👋

Unit 3   Learning the Language of Music   74

Unit Introduction

Element	Lesson	
EXPRESSION	**1** Accents!	78
	Arts Connection *Modern Painting with Clef*	
RHYTHM	**2** Hear a New Rhythm	80
	Movement: "Tideo"	
RHYTHM	**3** That Rhythm Again	82
	M★U★S★I★C M★A★K★E★R★S Franz Joseph Haydn	
	Show What You Know!	
RHYTHM	**4** Takes Two to Crawfish	86
	Movement: "Crawfish"	
	M★U★S★I★C M★A★K★E★R★S Papillion	
FORM	**5** What's the Form?	90
MELODY	**6** Water Melodies	92
MELODY	**7** Finding Patterns in Two Songs	94
MELODY	**8** Read a New Pitch	98
MELODY	**9** Sounds of the Sea	100
	Show What You Know!	
TIMBRE	**10** Colorful Sounds	102
	Listening Map: *Ujan mas*	
TEXTURE/HARMONY	**11** Creating Textures	106
TEXTURE/HARMONY	**12** Playing Lullaby Layers	108
REVIEW AND ASSESS	**Review, Assess, Perform, Create**	110

 = **Core Lesson**

 = **Music Reading Lesson**

Unit 4 Building Our Musical Skills   112

Unit Introduction
M*U*S*I*C M*A*K*E*R*S Carmen Miranda

Element	Lesson	
EXPRESSION	**1** Expressing the Weather	116
	Listening Map: *Saudação*	
RHYTHM	**2** Banjo Rhythms	120
	Arts **Connection** *The Banjo Lesson*	
RHYTHM	**3** Cooking with Rhythm	122
	Show What You Know!	
RHYTHM	**4** A Longer Sound	124
FORM	**5** Phrases That Move You!	126
	Movement: "A Song That's Just for You"	
MELODY	**6** Miles of Melody	128
	Movement: "How Many Miles to Babylon"	
MELODY	**7** Grow a Melody	130
MELODY	**8** A Flood of Sound	132
MELODY	**9** A Five-Pitch Song	134
	Show What You Know!	
TIMBRE	**10** String Sounds	138
	M*U*S*I*C M*A*K*E*R*S Eileen Ivers	
TEXTURE/HARMONY	**11** Turkish Textures	142
TEXTURE/HARMONY	**12** Music Among the Stars	144
	Arts **Connection** *Starry Night*	
REVIEW AND ASSESS	Review, Assess, Perform, Create	146

Core Lesson = ⭐
Music Reading Lesson = ✋

Unit 5 Discovering New Musical Horizons 148

Unit Introduction
Listening Map: *Fanfarre (Allegro Marziale)*
M★U★S★I★C M★A★K★E★R★S Joaquín Rodrigo

Element	Lesson	
EXPRESSION	**1** Connected Sounds—Separated Sounds	152

Movement: "Party Tonight!"

M★U★S★I★C M★A★K★E★R★S Steve Houghton

Movement: *Toccata and Tango*

RHYTHM	**2** Two Beats Long	156
RHYTHM	**3** Two Beats in One	158

Arts **Connection** *Jinshan Peasant Painting*

RHYTHM	**4** Elephant Rhythms	160

Listening Map: *Baby Elephant Walk*

Show What You Know!

FORM	**5** Questions and Answers	164
FORM	**6** Two Sections, Two Movements	166

Movement: "Sing a Rainbow"

MELODY	**7** A Melody to Sing—A Game to Play	170

Movement: "All Around the Buttercup"

MELODY	**8** Pentatonic Calypso	172
MELODY	**9** Singing for Fun!	174

Show What You Know!

TIMBRE	**10** Sounds of Dixieland	178

M★U★S★I★C M★A★K★E★R★S Louis Armstrong

TIMBRE	**11** Hear a Little Salsa	180
TEXTURE/HARMONY	**12** A New Kind of Ostinato	182
REVIEW AND ASSESS	Review, Assess, Perform, Create	184

 = Core Lesson
 = Music Reading Lesson

Unit 6 Making Music Our Own 186

Unit Introduction
M*U*S*I*C M*A*K*E*R*S Benny Goodman

Element	Lesson	
EXPRESSION	**1** Sing a Story	190
RHYTHM	**2** Rhythms in Three	192
RHYTHM	**3** Moving in Twos and Threes	194
	Movement: "Sleep, Baby, Sleep"	
RHYTHM	**4** One, Two, Three, Read!	198
	Show What You Know!	
FORM	**5** Sing It Again	200
	Poem: "Flies"	
FORM	**6** A Mountain of a Form	202
	M*U*S*I*C M*A*K*E*R*S Arthur Cunningham	
MELODY	**7** Pitches in the House	204
	Show What You Know!	
MELODY	**8** Melodic Ups and Downs	208
MELODY	**9** Melody Train	210
TIMBRE	**10** Plugged-in Sound	212
	M*U*S*I*C M*A*K*E*R*S Lydia Kavina	
	Listening Map: *Free Music #1*	
TEXTURE/HARMONY	**11** Lots and Lots of Layers	214
TEXTURE/HARMONY	**12** Create a Lion's Tale	216
	Story: "The Animals Find Water"	
REVIEW AND ASSESS	**Review, Assess, Perform, Create**	220

Core Lesson =

Music Reading Lesson =

Paths to Making Music

Unit 7   Music U.S.A.   224

Unit Introduction
Poem: "Way Down in the Music"

1 Friends Around the Country **228**
2 Games Americans Play **232**
   Movement: "Bob-a-Needle"
3 Singing on the Trail **234**
   Arts **Connection** *Untitled*
   Listening Map: *The Big Country*
4 Two American Styles **238**
   M*U*S*I*C M*A*K*E*R*S
   Ella Fitzgerald
5 Shining from the Inside . . . **240**

6 Express Yourself **242**
7 Texas Play-Party **244**
   Movement: "Shake Them
   'Simmons Down"
8 Music from Puerto Rico . . . **246**
9 Music of the First Americans **248**
10 Ragtime Rhythms **250**
11 Dancin' USA **252**
   M*U*S*I*C M*A*K*E*R*S
   Carlos Santana

Unit 8   Home and Away   256

Unit Introduction
Poem: "Around the World"

1 Getting There is Half
   the Fun! **260**
2 Hello, Friends! **262**
   M*U*S*I*C M*A*K*E*R*S
   Igor Stravinsky
3 Follow the Leader **266**
4 Do the Zudio! **268**
5 Singing Games
   Hawaiian Style **270**
6 Circle Around **272**
   Movement: "Ciranda"
   Arts **Connection** *Sally Walker*

7 Let's Play the Drum! **274**
8 Chinese Timbres **276**
9 Dancing Across the Ages . . **278**
   Arts **Connection** *Court Ball at
   the Palais du Louvre*
   Listening Map: *Pavane et
   Gaillarde*
   Movement: *Patty Cake Polka*
10 Play-Party **282**
11 A Maori Goodbye **284**
12 Sing Your Way Home **286**

Unit 9 Creature Feature 288

Unit Introduction
M★U★S★I★C M★A★K★E★R★S The Banana Slug String Band

1 Frog Music 292
2 Sounds of Nature 294
3 Creature Tale 296
   Story: "Chawe chidyo chem'chero"
4 Cat Music 300
5 A Batty Melody 302
6 Rabbit Rhythms 304
   Poem: "Rabbits"

7 Crabby Lullaby 306
   Arts Connection *Untitled*
8 A Musical Menagerie 308
9 Worms at Work! 310
   Movement: *Disco Worm*
10 Pluckin' Patterns 314
   Arts Connection
   The Banjo Lesson

Unit 10 Our Planet Earth 316

Unit Introduction
Poem: "Breaks Free"

1 A New Day 320
2 Sing for the Trees 322
   M★U★S★I★C M★A★K★E★R★S
   Sharon Burch
3 Music of the Wind 324
   Movement: "Who Has Seen the Wind?"
   Poem: "To a Red Kite"
4 Move with the Rain 328
5 Dance a Wonderful Day! . . 330
   Movement: "Zip-a-Dee-Doo-Dah"

6 Sing a Rainbow! 332
7 Play into the Sunset 334
   Arts Connection *Sunsets*
8 Star Textures 336
   M★U★S★I★C M★A★K★E★R★S
   Amy Beach
   Listening Map: *Sous les étoiles*
9 Music for a Comet 340
   M★U★S★I★C M★A★K★E★R★S
   Mary Chapin Carpenter
10 Care for the Ocean 342
11 The Oceans of the Earth . . . 344

Unit 11 **Perform a Story**   346

Unit Introduction
M*U*S*I*C M*A*K*E*R*S George Frideric Handel
Listening Map: *The Arrival of the Queen of Sheba*

1 Sing a Dragon Tale 350
2 Jabuti's Song Saves
   the Day 352
   Story: "Kibungo, Beast of
   the Forest"
3 Sing a Legend 356
   Poem: "The Stars Streaming
   in the Sky"
4 Sounds of a Train 358

5 A Song that Grows! 360
6 Sing a Funny Story 362
   Poem: "How Doth the
   Little Crocodile"
7 Cajun Crocodile Song 364
8 Dancing Animals 366
9 A Story with a Moral 368
   Story: "Yertle the Turtle"

Unit 12 **Celebrate the Season**   372

Unit Introduction

1 Fiesta Time! 374
2 Ooooooh! It's Halloween! . . 376
3 Harvest Time 378
4 Celebrate Thanksgiving . . . 380
   Poem: "Setting the Thanksgiving
   Table"
5 Chanukah, the Festival
   of Lights 382
6 Celebrate Christmas 384
7 A Christmas Waltz 386
   Arts **Connection** The Skater
   Movement: *Les patineurs*

8 Winter Fun! 388
   Arts **Connection**
   Holiday Sleigh Ride
   M*U*S*I*C M*A*K*E*R*S
   Leroy Anderson
9 Celebrate Kwanzaa 392
10 Living the Dream 394
   Poem: "When I Grow Up"
11 Valentine's Day! 398
12 Celebrate Spring 400
13 Celebrate America! 402
   Arts **Connection**
   The Continentals

Music Resources

Music Reading Practice 406
Mallet Instruments 418
Sound Bank 420
Glossary 426

Classified Index 428
Credits 432
Index of Songs and
Speech Pieces 434

STEPS TO
Making
Music

Let the Good Times Begin!

Anyone can make music. You can sing, move, play, listen to, and create music. Get ready to begin making music!

Let the Music Begin!

Songs That Entertain

Bill Shontz wrote this song. Sometimes he works with his partner, Gary Rosen. They call themselves Rosenshontz.

Move in cool ways as you **listen** to "Gonna Have a Good Time."

Gonna Have a Good Time

Words and Music by Bill Shontz

VERSE

1. Lis - ten to the sound of the mu - sic,
2. Lis - ten to the sound of the mu - sic,

Lis - ten to the sound of the flute;
Lis - ten to the sound of the drums;

Lis - ten to the sound of the mu - sic,
Lis - ten to the sound of the mu - sic,

Fine

Gon - na have a good time. ____

Visit **Take it to the Net** at *www.sfsuccessnet.com* to find out more about Rosenshontz.

REFRAIN

Come on,   let's   go,   one,   two,   three;
Come on,   let's   go,   sev'n,   eight,   nine;

You're the   on - ly   one   so   dance _   with   me;
When you   dance with   me,   I   feel ___   so   fine;

Come   on,   let's   go,   four,   five,   six;
Come   on,   let's   go,   ten,   'leven,   twelve;

D.C. al Fine

If   you   don't   dance,   I'm   in   a   fix. ___
If   you   don't   dance,   I'll   dance   my - self. ___

3. Listen to the sound of the saxophone,
    Listen to the sound of the beat!
    Listen to the sound of the saxophone,
    Gonna have a good time!
    (Fine)

LOUD AND SOFT SOUNDS = DYNAMICS!

Music around us can be loud or soft. Look at the pictures below. Imagine the sounds you might hear. Describe the **dynamics** to a partner.

Dynamics is a word that describes the loudness or softness of music.

Using Dynamics

Listen to the loud and soft parts in this song.

Now **sing** the song.

CD 1–3
MIDI 1

Heigh-Ho

from *Snow White and the Seven Dwarfs*

Words by Larry Morey   *Music by Frank Churchill*

"Heigh-ho,   heigh-ho," To make your trou-bles go,
        ho,   heigh-ho," It's home from work we go,

just keep on sing - ing all day long "Heigh-ho,
(whistle or hum) _____ "Heigh-ho,

heigh - ho, heigh - ho, heigh - ho,   heigh - ho,"
heigh - ho, heigh - ho, heigh - ho,   heigh - ho,"

For if you're feel-ing low,   You pos - i - tive - ly can't go wrong
All sev - en   in a row,   (whistle or hum) _____

With a "heigh,   heigh - ho heigh - ho, heigh -
With a "heigh,   heigh -   -ho."

THE BEAT GOES ON

Most music has a **steady beat.** There are many ways to keep the beat. As you **listen** to the song, **clap** to keep the beat.

A **steady beat** is the regular pulse found in most music.

CD 1–5

Time to Sing

Words and Music by Raffi, D. Pike, and B. & B. Simpson

VERSE

G

1. It's time to sing a song or two.

Am₇ D₇

You with me and me with you. ___

Last time to Coda

G E₇ Am₇ D₇ G

Time for us to sing a - while, . Hey, hey, hey.

REFRAIN

C C#dim G

And it's time for say - ing hi and hel - lo.

A₇ D₇ *D.C. al Coda*

Let's all sing a song that we know.

Coda

Am7 D7   G   E7   Am7   D7   G   E7

Hey, hey, hey, I'm sing-ing, Hey, hey, hey, we're sing-ing

Am7   D7   G

Hey, _____ hey, ___ hey, _ hey.

2. It's time for us to clap our hands
   in rhythm with the beat.
   Time for hands to clap awhile,
   Hey, hey, hey. *Refrain*

3. It's time for us to tap our toes
   together with our feet.
   Time for toes to tap awhile,
   Hey, hey, hey. *Refrain*

4. It's time to make a sound you like,
   la la la . . . .
   Refrain, then repeat Verse 1 to Coda

Moving to the Beat

Move to show the steady beat as you **sing** the song. How many different ways can you keep a steady beat?

Rhythm of the Words

Music has steady beats. It also has **rhythm. Clap** the rhythm of the words of "Time to Sing."

Tap Dance Rhythms

Tap dancers make exciting rhythms with their feet. They wear special shoes with metal tips at the toes and heels.

Liam Burke is a member of *Tap Dogs*. **Listen** to the rhythm of his tap dancing.

CD 1–7
Interview with Liam Burke

MUSIC MAKERS

TAP DOGS

Tap Dogs is a stage show from Australia. It is part tap dance and part rock concert. The dancers wear work boots. They dance on steel, on wood floors, and on electronic drum pads.

Get the Rhythm

Sing this song as you **pat** the steady beat. **Sing** the song again and **clap** the rhythm of the words.

CD 1–8
MIDI 2

GO AROUND THE CORN, SALLY

African American Work Song

Go a-round, round and round, Go a-round the corn, Sal-ly.

Hey now, Hey ___ now, Go a-round the corn, Sal-ly.

Fast-er still, Fast-er still, Round and round the corn, Sal-ly.

All a-round, all a-round, Go a-round the corn, Sal-ly.

Find a partner. One claps the rhythm as the other pats a steady beat. Sometimes one claps two times when the other pats only once.

One and Two Sounds on a Beat

Tap the corn as you **say** the words.

> Go   a -   round,   'round and   'round

The notes below show the rhythm. **Tap** the rhythm.

Go a -   round,   'round and   'round

Find the ears of corn that have one sound.

One sound on a beat

Then find the ears of corn that have two sounds.

Two sounds on a beat

Rhythms at Rest

Listen to this song from China. At the end of each line, there is one beat with no sound.

CD 1–13

Xiao yin chuan
(Silver Moon Boat)

Folk Song from China

Yue   er   wan wan xiang   yi   tiao chuan   gua   tian shang
Lit - tle   sil - ver   moon   rides the   sky   like   a   boat,

Chuan guo xing xing   ta   yi   ran   qing   ying piao dang
Past   the   twink-ling   stars   it   will float,   light - ly   float.

Yang   fan ___   xiang   zhe   xi   fang   hang
Sail,   lit - tle   moon   boat,   to   the   west,

Jia   xiao xiao yin   chuan   duo   an   xiang.
Sail,   lit - tle   moon   boat,   while   I   rest.

No Sound on the Beat

Find these rhythms in the song.

- One sound on the beat = ♩
- Two sounds on the beat = ♫
- No sounds on the beat = 𝄽 (rest)

Find the sailboat below with the 𝄽.

Jia

xiao xiao

yin

chuan

duo

an

xiang

Now **play** this pattern as you sing the song.

Rhythm Fun!

This little bird from Spain sings a special song.
Find what the bird sings. Then **tap** the rhythm.

 CD 1–20

Un pajarito
(A Little Bird)

English Words by Alice Firgau   *Folk Song from Spain*

En   la   pun - ta   del   man - za - no
From   the   tree - top   of   the   ap - ple

hay   un   pa - ja - ri - to,   un   pa - ja - ri - to,
tree   a   lit - tle   bird   sings,   A   lit - tle   bird   sings,

que   sin   ce - sar   siem - pre   can - ta a - sì.
Sings   al - ways sweet - ly   the   whole   day   long.

Chi - ru - li - ru - li!   Chi - ru - li - ru - li
Chi - ru - li - ru - li!   Chi - ru - li - ru - li!

can - ta, pa - ja - ri - to, can - ta y siem-pre can - ta a - sì.
Lit - tle bird, come sing your song, so sweet-ly   all day long.

16

Rhythm Patterns

Sing the song again. Find this rhythm pattern in the song.

Chi - ru - li - ru - li

Rhythm syllables are used to name specific rhythmic units.

Using **rhythm syllables, say** the pattern. What other patterns can you find in the song?

Show What You Know!

These rhythm patterns are from songs you know. First **clap** or **pat** each pattern. Then name the song.

1.

2.

3.

Create your own rhythm pattern using

, and ♪.

Clap or **pat** your pattern. **Play** it on an instrument.

Let the Spirit Move You

Listen to "Michael, Row the Boat Ashore."

CD 1–24   Michael, Row the Boat Ashore

African American Spiritual

1. Mi - chael, row the boat a - shore,
2. Sis - ter help to trim the sail,

Hal - le - lu - jah!
Hal - le - lu - jah!

Mi - chael, row the boat a - shore,
Sis - ter help to trim the sail.

Hal - le - lu - jah!
Hal - le - lu - jah!

3. River Jordan's deep and wide, . . .   4. Trumpet sound the jubilee, . . .
   Milk and honey on the other side. . . .   Cross this riv'r and we'll be free. . . .

Call and Response

Did you notice that first one person sings the **call,** then a group sings the **response?**

Get in the Boat and Move!

Take your place in the "boat" and **sing** the song. Use your rhythm sticks as oars during the call parts. **Tap** the floor on the beat.

During the response raise the sticks into the air. **Tap** them together as you sway from side to side on the beat.

Element: MELODY | **Skill: LISTENING** | **Connection: SOCIAL STUDIES**

Up and Down the Music Trail

Cowboys spent long days and nights moving cattle along the dusty trail. They sang songs to make their work easier. They also sang to pass the time in the evenings.

Sing this cowboy song. Find the high and low **pitches.**

Pitch is another word for a musical note. Pitch is how high or low a note sounds.

CD 1–26

Lone Star Trail

Cowboy Song from the United States

VERSE

1. I start-ed on the trail on June twen-ty-third,
I been punch-in' Tex-as cat-tle on the Lone Star Trail;

REFRAIN

Sing-in' ki yi yip-pi yip-pi yay, yip-pi yay!

Sing-in' ki yi yip-pi yip-pi yay! _____

2. I'm up in the mornin' before daylight,
   And before I sleep the moon shines bright. *Refrain*

3. Oh, it's bacon and beans 'most every day,
   I'd as soon be a-eatin' prairie hay. *Refrain*

4. My feet are in the stirrups and my rope is on the side,
   Show me a horse that I can't ride. *Refrain*

Moving High, Moving Low

Listen to "Lone Star Trail."

Move up and down to show the high and low pitches. Pretend you are riding a horse.

Play Along

Now **play** these patterns while the class sings.

M·U·S·I·C M·A·K·E·R·S

Aaron Copland

Aaron Copland (1900–1990) was an American composer whose music is very popular. He began writing songs when he was eight years old. He started writing an opera when he was only eleven.

22

Cowboys on Holiday

Listen to *Buckaroo Holiday* as you follow the listening map. The knots on the rope show how the pitches move from high to low.

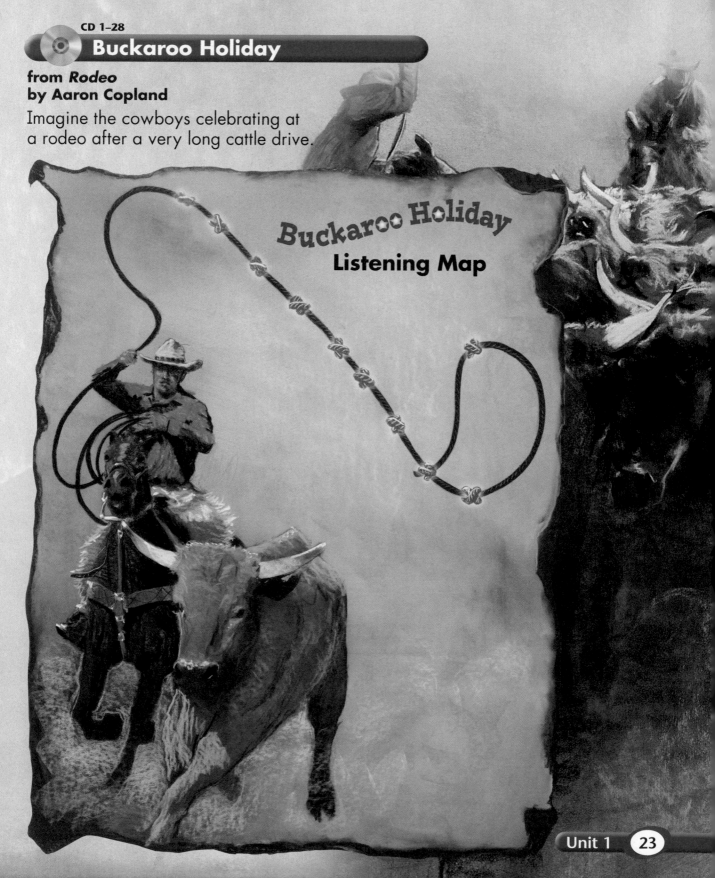

CD 1–28

Buckaroo Holiday

**from *Rodeo*
by Aaron Copland**

Imagine the cowboys celebrating at a rodeo after a very long cattle drive.

Buckaroo Holiday
Listening Map

Element: MELODY | **Skill: SINGING** | **Connection: STYLE**

Follow the Direction

Listen to "My Father's House."
Trace the direction of the **melody.**

Melody is a row of pitches that move up or down or repeat.

Won't you come
with
me_____ to my
fa-
ther's
house, ____

house? ____
house,_____ ther's
To my fa- ther's to my fa-

Won't you come
with
me _____ to my
fa-
ther's
house, ____

peace, _____
is peace, _____
There peace._____

of the MUSIC

Now **sing** the song. **Move** your hand
to show the direction of the melody.

 CD 1–29

My Father's House

Traditional Song from the Southern United States

1.–3.   Won't you come with me   to   my   fa-ther's house,

To   my   fa-ther's house,   to   my   fa-ther's house?

Won't you   come with   me   to   my   fa-ther's house,

1. There   is   peace,   peace,   peace.
2. There   is   joy,   joy,   joy.
3. There   is   love,   love,   love.

Three Pitches

"Lucy Locket" is a singing game. The song has only the three pitches—*so*, *mi*, and *la*.

These are the hand signs.

so   mi   la

Singing with Pitch Syllables

The first pitch of the song is *so.* **Sing** "Lucy Locket" with **pitch syllables.** Then add the hand signs.

Pitch syllables are used to name pitches, for example, *so, mi,* and *la.*

CD 1–32

Lucy Locket

Street Rhyme

so

Lu - cy Lock - et   lost her pock - et. Kit - ty Fish - er found   it.

Not   a   pen - ny was there in   it. On - ly   rib - bon 'round   it.

Pitches are written on a five-line staff.

 ← **staff**

Sometimes *so, mi,* and *la* are in different places on the staff. On this staff, *so* is in the third space.

so

Where are *mi* and *la?*

Read Pizza, Play Pizza

Find *so, mi,* and *la* in "Pizza, Pizza, Daddy-o."

 CD 1-36

Pizza, Pizza, Daddy-o

Singing Game from the United States

Solo

Jim - my's got a girl - friend,

Chorus

Piz - za, piz - za, Dad - dy - o, How do you know it?

Chorus

Piz - za, piz - za, Dad - dy - o, 'Cause he told me,

Chorus

Piz - za, piz - za, Dad - dy - o, Let's rope it,

◀ *Children Playing London Bridge* by William H. Johnson

"London Bridge," like "Pizza, Pizza, Daddy-o," is a singing game. Children play games like these in playgrounds, in schoolyards, and on sidewalks.

Chorus rope it, rope __ it, Dad - dy - o, *Solo* Let's swim it,

Chorus swim it, swim __ it, Dad - dy - o, *Solo* Let's duck it,

Chorus duck it, duck __ it, Dad - dy - o, *Solo* Let's twist it,

Chorus twist it, twist __ it, Dad - dy - o, *Solo* Let's end it,

Chorus End it, end __ it, Dad - dy - o.

The Pizza Pizza Game

Play this game as you **sing** "Pizza, Pizza, Daddy-o." First the leader sings. Then the whole group answers.

You can **create** your own verses for this game.

Beat 1   Beat 2   Beat 3   Beat 4

Hold beat 6 position.

Beat 5   Beat 6   Beat 7   Beat 8

Show What You Know!

Remember that *so, mi,* and *la* can be in different places on the staff. On the staff below, *so* is in the third space. Where are *mi* and *la*?

so   ?   ?

Show where each of these pitch syllable patterns would go on a staff. Start with *so* in the third space.

1. so so la la so mi

2. so so mi la so so

You Are the Music

You can make music without an instrument.
Listen carefully to "Down, Down, Baby."
Which sounds are like instruments but really
performed with parts of the body?

When you make music like this, it is called
body percussion.

CD 1–41
MIDI 3

Swing style

Down, Down, Baby

African American Clapping Song

1. Down, down, ba-by, down,___ down a rol-ler coast-er,

Sweet, sweet ba-by, I___ love a rol-ler coast-er;

Shim-my, shim-my, co-coa pop, shim-my, shim-my, pop,___

All to-geth-er with the chick-ens and the feath-ers.

32

Warren Smith is a musician and hambone artist. Hamboning is a style of body percussion. ▼

P - O - P spells pop, oh, my hon - ey,

P - O - P spells pop, oh, my ba - by,

P - O - P spells POP!

2. Down, down, baby, down, down a roller coaster,
Sweet, sweet baby, I love a roller coaster;
Shimmy, shimmy, cocoa pop, shimmy, shimmy pop.
Grandma, Grandmama, sick in bed,
Called the doctor and the doctor said,
"Let's get the motion of the head, ding dong,
Let's get the motion of the hands, clap clap,
Let's get the motion of the feet, stomp stomp,
Put it all together and what do you get?
Ding dong, clap clap, stomp stomp.
Say it all backwards and what do you get?
Stomp stomp, clap clap, ding dong!"

Thin to Thick

Chirp, Chirp

Perform this rhyme to a steady beat.

CD 1–43
MIDI 4

RIDDLE REE

Words and Rhythmic Setting by Grace Nash

Rid - dle, rid - dle, rid - dle, ree, do what I do af - ter me.

Stamp, clap, stamp, clap. Sway, sway.

Touch your toes, touch your nose, 'round in cir - cles each one goes.

Bow once, bow twice, bend down low and plant some rice.

Lift your hands up to the sky, shake them out and hold them high.

Clap your hands, stamp your feet, cym - bals crash and that's com - plete!

Adding Sounds

Add this **ostinato** as the class performs "Riddle Ree."

An **ostinato** is a short repeated pattern.

Rid - dle me this and rid - dle me that!

Then add this ostinato.

Slide slide to the far side.

When one person speaks alone, the sound is thin. When more people join in, the sound gets thicker.

Review, Assess,

What Do You Know?

1. Read the notation for "Lucy Locket" on page 27.

   a. Find four words in the song that are sung on *so*.

   b. Find four words that are sung on *la*.

   c. Find three words that are sung on *mi*.

2. Match the following words with their meanings.

   a. *forte* (*f*)　　• soft

   b. *piano* (*p*)　　• changes in loudness and softness

   c. dynamics　　• loud

What Do You Hear? 1

CD 1–45

Listen to the dynamics in each piece. Circle the words that describe the music.

   1. mostly loud　　mostly soft
   2. mostly loud　　mostly soft
   3. mostly loud　　mostly soft
   4. mostly loud　　mostly soft

Perform, Create

What You Can Do

Sing a Pattern

Sing each of the following patterns and indicate the placement of notes on the finger staff:

a. so

b. so

Create a Rhythm

Create a body percussion part to play as you sing "Lone Star Trail." Start by imitating the sound of horses' hooves. Use only ♩, ♫, and 𝄽.

Create a Melody

Work with a partner to create your own call-and-response song.

- Clap each of the rhythms below.

a.

b.

- Use *so, mi,* and *la* to create a melody to go with each rhythm.

- Perform one melody as a call while your partner performs the other melody as the response.

Dance to the Music

What different ways do you explore music? Some music makes you want to dance. **Listen** to *Liberty/Chicken Reel* and identify when the music changes. Then **move** to the music. **Create** movements that show when the music changes.

CD 2–1
Liberty/Chicken Reel
Traditional

Some of the instruments you will hear are pennywhistle, fiddle, and hammered dulcimer.

Exploring Music

A Rockin' Rhythm

Sing and **move** to this song.

CD 2-2

The Music's in Me

Words and Music by Jill Gallina

VERSE

1. When I hear mu - sic, mu-sic with a rock-in' beat, _
2. When I hear mu - sic, mu-sic with a rock-in' beat, _

my hands start clap - pin', my toes start tap - pin',
my heart starts thump - in', my blood starts pump - in',

I've got-ta move my feet. _ I love that rhy - thm.
I've got-ta move my feet. _ I love that rhy - thm.

I could nev-er get my fill, __ 'cause when I hear that
There's noth-in' like a rock-in' song. _ And when I hear that

mu - sic play, _ you know that I just can't sit still. __
mu - sic play, _ you know I've got - ta sing a - long __

REFRAIN

The mu-sic's in me. _ It keeps me rock-in' you see. _

The mu-sic's in me. _ It keeps me rock-in' you see. _

Creating Music

Listen to the song again. Then **create** a rhythm pattern to play along with the recording. What instrument will you **play**?

"Speed Up," Slow Down

Sing "Miss Mary Mack" at different speeds, or **tempos.**

Tempo is the speed of the beat in music.

CD 2–4
MIDI 5

Miss Mary Mack

African American Clapping Game Song

1. Miss Ma - ry Mack, Mack, Mack,

All dressed in black, black, black,

With sil - ver but-tons, but-tons, but-tons,

All down her back, back, back.

2. She asked her mother,
     mother, mother,
   For fifteen cents, cents, cents,
   To see the elephants,
     elephants, elephants
   Jump over the fence, fence, fence.

3. They jumped so high,
     high, high,
   They touched the sky, sky, sky,
   And never came down,
     down, down,
   'Til the fourth of July, 'ly, 'ly.

Game Time

Play this game with a partner.

Step 4

1. Cross your arms, hands on shoulders.

2. Pat your thighs.

3. Clap your hands.

4. Clap your partner's right hand.

5. Clap your hands.

Step 8

6. Clap your partner's left hand.

7. Clap your hands.

8. Clap both of your partner's hands.

Arts Connection

▲ *Untitled* by Keith Haring (1958–1990). Haring created bright, exciting paintings. How does this painting show movement?

Frog Rhythms

This song has 𝅘𝅥, 𝅘𝅥𝅘𝅥, and 𝄽. **Sing** "Frog in the Millpond" and look for these rhythms.

CD 2–8

Frog in the Millpond

Additional Verses by Bryan Louiselle   *Traditional Song from the United States*

1. Frog in the mill - pond, Can't get him out.

Take a lit - tle stick and stir him a - bout.

2. Frog in the millpond,
   Hops pretty quick.
   Better use a net;
   He doesn't like the stick.

3. Frog in the millpond,
   Hides in the muck.
   Broke out of the net
   with froggie kind of luck.

Feel the Rhythm

Tap a steady beat on each lily pad as you **sing** the last line of the song. Then clap the words to feel the rhythm.

stir   him   a -   bout

Stir Up the Rhythm

The rhythms to the first line of the song are stirred up here. Can you find the line that matches the song?

Create a Frog Rhythm

Create your own frog rhythm using ♩, ♫ , and 𝄽.

Move to show the rhythm you created.

Perform your frog rhythms on rhythm sticks for the class.

Element: RHYTHM | **Skill: PLAYING** | **Connection: RELATED ARTS**

 Pick a

Sing "Four in a Boat." Which lines have the same rhythm pattern?

CD 2–13

Four in a Boat

Play-Party Song from Appalachia

1. Four in a boat and the tide rolls high,

Four in a boat and the tide rolls high,

Four in a boat and the tide rolls high,

Wait-ing for a pret - ty one to come bye and bye.

2. Choose your partner and stay all day, . . .
We don't care what the old folks say.

3. Eight in a boat and it won't go 'round, . . .
Swing that pretty one that you just found.

Pattern

Play a Pattern!

Say this rhythm pattern using rhythm syllables.
Then **play** the rhythm on an instrument.

Rhythm in Art

Find the patterns in this painting. Why do you think it is called *Rhythmical*?

Arts Connection

▲ *Rhythmical* by Paul Klee (1879–1940)

Piano Patterns

Listen to *Allegro non troppo* by Béla Bartók.
Find two rhythm patterns that are different.
Move to show fast and slow.

CD 2–20

 Allegro non troppo, No. 33

**from *For Children (Sz 42), Volume II*
by Béla Bartók**

Bártok wrote these pieces especially for young children
to play on the piano.

Show What You Know!

Clap these rhythms. Find the patterns
that repeat.

1.

2.

3.

4.

Get on the BEAT

Sing this song. Try to *step it down* on the **strong beats.**

The **strong beat** is the most important beat in a rhythm pattern.

CD 2–21

Way Down in the Schoolyard

Traditional
New Words and Musical Arrangement
by Sharon, Lois, and Bram

Swing Style
REFRAIN

Way   down   yon - der   in   the   school - yard,

re - mem - ber   me?

Way   down   yon - der   in   the   school - yard,

Fine (after verse 3)

re - mem - ber   me.

Move It, Groove It!

Listen to the original version of the song.
Move on the strong beats.

CD 2–23

Way Down Yonder in the Brickyard

Traditional African American

Bessie Jones and the Georgia Sea Island Singers made this recording in 1979.

VERSE

1. Well step it, step it, step it ___ down, _

re - mem - ber me? _____ You got - ta

step it, step it, step it ___ down, _

re - mem - ber me.

2. Now twirl your sweetheart, twirl her (him) now,
   Remember me?
   You gotta twirl your sweetheart, twirl him (her) now,
   Remember me. *(Repeat)*
   Refrain

3. Now find another, find him (her) now,
   Remember me?
   You gotta find another, find him (her) now,
   Remember me. *(Repeat)*
   Refrain

SINGIN' THE BLUES

The blues is a way for people to express their feelings through music. **Sing** this blues song with feeling.

Form is the order of same and different ideas in music.

"Good Mornin', Blues" has two different musical ideas, **a** and **b**. The order of these ideas is called **form.** What is the form of this song?

CD 2–24

GOOD MORNIN', BLUES

Edited and New Additional Material by Alan Lomax

New Words and New Music Arranged by Huddie Ledbetter

1. Good morn - in', blues,   Blues, how do   you   do?

Good morn - in', blues,   Blues, how do   you   do?

I'm   do-in' all right, ___ Good morn-in', how are you?

TRO - © Copyright 1959 (renewed) Folkways Music Publishers, Inc., New York, NY. Used with permission.

HUDDIE LEDBETTER

Huddie "Leadbelly" Ledbetter (1885–1949) was a well-known blues singer and guitar player. Leadbelly is in the Blues Hall of Fame *and* the Rock and Roll Hall of Fame.

Can't Get Enough of the Blues

Listen to the melody of this blues song. It is sung by Huddie Ledbetter. Is it in **a a b** form?

CD 2–26

When a Man's a Long Way from Home

Traditional Blues Song

Huddie Ledbetter said he could sing and play more than 500 different songs.

Singing Ecuador

Sing this song that children in Ecuador enjoy. Look for pitch patterns with *so*, *mi*, and *la*.

CD 2–27

El juego chirimbolo
(The *Chirimbolo* Game)

English Words by Alice Firgau   *Singing Game from Ecuador*

El   jue - go chi - rim - bo - lo,. ¡qué bo - ni - to es!
This   game is chi - rim - bo - lo;   Play and you'll have fun.

Con un pie,   o - tro pie,   u - na ma - no, o - tra ma - no,
First one foot,   oth - er foot;   Then one hand, __ oth - er   hand; __

un   co - do,   o - tro co - do.   El   co - do,
One el - bow,   oth - er el - bow.   This el - bow.

El   jue - go chi - rim - bo - lo,   ¡qué bo - ni - to es!   ¡Hey!
We're play-ing chi - rim - bo - lo. Now the game is done.   Hey!

Play a Game

Play the *chirimbolo* game with classmates.
The words of the song tell you how to move.

Ecuador is a country on the continent of South America. ▶

 Video Library Watch *Singing Games*. This video shows singing games from the United States, Mexico, Japan, and Ghana.

Find a New Pitch

Sing this song using *so, mi,* and *la.* **Listen** for a new pitch at the end. Is the new pitch higher or lower than *so, mi,* and *la?*

CD 2–32

Clouds of Gray

Words and Music by Katinka S. Daniel

la

so

mi

?

1. Clouds of gray are in the sky,
2. Lit - tle flow - ers down - ward creep,

Flocks of birds are pass - ing by,
Nod their drow - sy heads and sleep,

Trees now dress in fad - ed brown,
All the world must say "good night,"

Send their leaves all rust - ling down.
Till spring comes with sun - shine bright.

| la | so | mi | ? |

New Pitch—New Sign

As you **sing** the song, show hand signs for *la*, *so*, *mi*, and the new pitch. Hum the new pitch.

Sing an Autumn Poem

Sing this poem, using the melody from "Clouds of Gray."

Wind Has Shaken Autumn Down

by Tony Johnston

Wind has shaken autumn down,
left it sprawling on the ground,
shawling all in gold below,
waiting for the hush of snow.

NAME THE NEW PITCH

Sing this moon song. Find *so* and *mi* on the staff. *So* and *mi* are in spaces. Where is the new pitch?

CD 2–37

I SEE THE MOON

Melody by Denise Bacon, Adapted

I   see   the   moon   and   the

moon   sees   me.

Moon   sees   some - bod - y

I   want   to   see.

What Is the Name?

The new pitch is called *do*.

Sing "I See the Moon," using *so, mi,* and *do*.
Point to each pitch on the staff.

Show What You Know!

Sing these patterns using pitch syllables.

1. do

2. do

3. do

Tune In

Sometimes the moon seems very large and close. It is really more than 230,000 miles from earth.

MELODIC

Every melody moves in its own direction.
Sing this song and trace the path of the melody.

CD 2–42

Down the Ohio

River Shanty

VERSE

The riv - er is up and the chan - nel is deep,

The wind is stead - y and strong.

1. Oh, won't we have a jol - ly good time
2. The waves do splash from shore ___ to shore

As we go sail - ing a - long.

PATHWAYS

Follow the Path of a Melody

Find where the pitches repeat,
where the pitches skip,
and where the pitches step.

REFRAIN

Down the riv - er, Oh, down the riv - er,

Oh, down the riv - er we go. _____

Down the riv - er, Oh, down the riv - er,

Oh, down the O - hi - o!

CD-ROM Create your own melody with *Making Music* software. Use steps, skips, and repeated pitches.

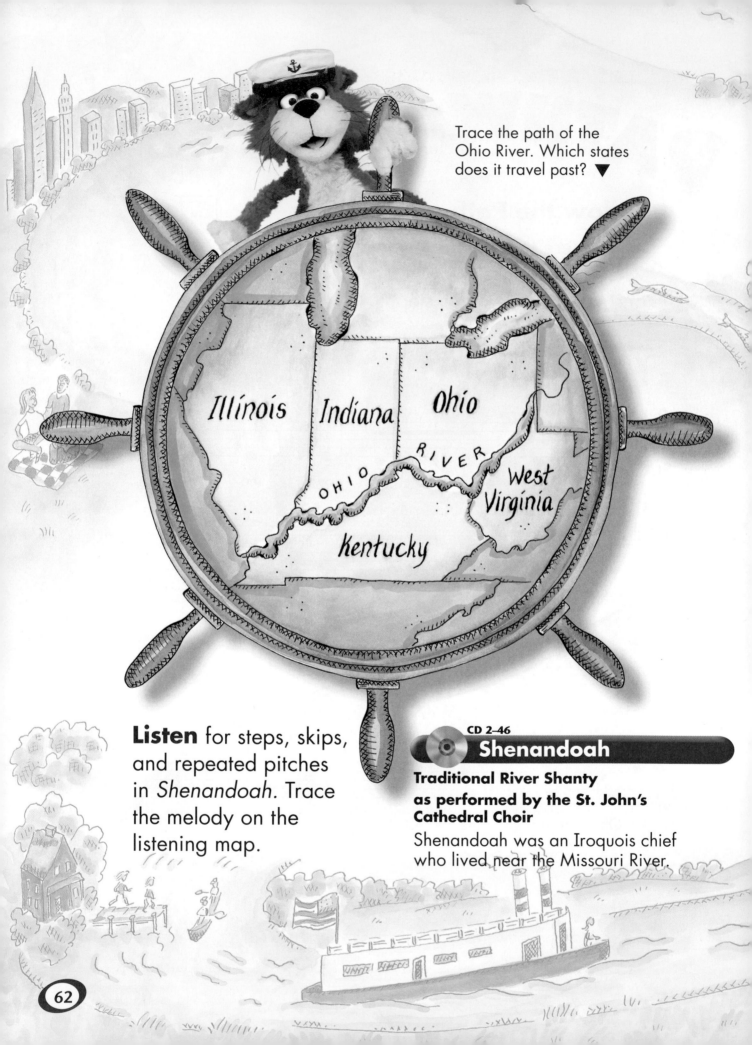

Trace the path of the Ohio River. Which states does it travel past? ▼

Illinois Indiana Ohio

OHIO RIVER

West Virginia

Kentucky

Listen for steps, skips, and repeated pitches in *Shenandoah*. Trace the melody on the listening map.

CD 2–46

Shenandoah

Traditional River Shanty
as performed by the St. John's Cathedral Choir

Shenandoah was an Iroquois chief who lived near the Missouri River.

shenandoah Listening Map

Percussion

The way an instrument is made gives it a special sound, or **timbre.**

Sing this song from Israel. **Listen** for the timbre of the tambourine.

> **Timbre** is the special sound each instrument makes.

CD 3–1

Achshav
(Awake! Awake!)

English Words by David Eddleman

Folk Song from Israel

Ach - shav,   ach - shav,   b' - em - ek   Yis - ra - el;
A - wake!   A - wake!   the   val - leys   of   our   land,

Ach - shav,   ach - shav,   b' - em - ek   Yis - ra - el.
A - wake!   A - wake!   the   val - leys   of   our   land.

Tum - ba, tum - ba, tum - ba,   b' - em - ek Yis - ra - el,   Hey!
Tum - ba, tum - ba, tum - ba,   the   land of   Is - ra - el,   Hey!

Tum - ba, tum - ba, tum - ba,   b' - em - ek Yis - ra - el,   Hey!
Tum - ba, tum - ba, tum - ba,   the   land of   Is - ra - el,   Hey!

Timbres

Tambourine Techniques

Tambourines are played using different **techniques.** They can be tapped or shaken. **Play** these tambourine patterns with "*Achshav.*"

Technique is the special skill used to play an instrument.

(val - leys   of   our   land)

(shake)

(Is - ra - el,   Hey!)

A World of Drums

Listen to this recording of drums. Different drums have different timbres. Can you tell which drums are being played? **Describe** what you hear.

CD 3–6
World of Drums Montage

▲ Tabla player from India

▲ Timpani player

▼ *Taiko* drum players

▲ Drum set player

Who Is the Drum?

Listen to this poem.
Who is the narrator
of the poem?

CD 3–7

De Beat

by Grace Nichols

The poet is a native of British Guiana.

▲ *Djembe* player

De Beat
by Grace Nichols

De beat of de drum
    is a living heart
De skin of de drum
    is a living goat
De wood of de drum
    is a living tree
De belly of de drum
    is de call of de sea
De dum of de drum
    is me

Speaking in Layers

Children in West Africa learn to drum when they are about seven years old. They chant words to help them learn the patterns.

Combine these names of African tribes in different ways. Say the names over and over in rhythm. This **creates** an ostinato.

Ibo   *Ashanti*   *Hausa*
Fon   *Yoruba*   *Kotokoli*

Performing in Layers

Perform your ostinato with the ostinato of a classmate. **Create** a thicker sound by adding more ostinatos.

Hear the Layers

Listen for the layers of repeating patterns in *Oya*.

CD 3–8

Oya

**from *Primitive Fire*
by Babatunde Olatunji**

Some of the instruments you will hear are *shekere*, *gankogui*, and *djembe*.

M·U·S·I·C M·A·K·E·R·S

Babatunde Olatunji

Babatunde Olatunji (1927–2003) was a well-known drummer from Nigeria. In the 1960s he brought the sounds of Nigerian drumming and chanting to the United States.

Play a Musical Message

Sing this story song from Ghana. Ghana is a country in West Africa.

Ayelivi is a girl who goes to pick berries for her mother and gets lost in the jungle. The friendly animals help her find her way home.

CD 3–9
MIDI 6

Ayelivi

*Story Song from Ghana
Arranged by Komla Amoaku*

Solo

A - ye - li - vi ___ no ku - do mi do
A - ye - li - vi ___ has lost her way and

ba ba ___ n'a - ye - li - vi.
can't find ___ her moth - er dear.

Chorus

Yie yie mi do ba ba ___ n'a - ye - li - vi.
Wah, wah, we feel sad for ___ A - ye - li - vi.

Building Texture

Play these rhythms one at a time. Then play them together in layers to create a thicker **texture.**

Texture is how thin or thick the music sounds.

Perform the Story

Play your music with the story about Ayelivi.

Story songs are used throughout Africa. They teach children important lessons about life.

Review, Assess,

What Do You Know?

1. How do the pitches below move? Match the music with the correct word.

a.

• step

b.

• repeated pitches

c.

• skip

2. Name the pitches in the staff below.

do

mi

What Do You Hear? 2

CD 3–13

You will hear three pairs of musical examples. Decide which word or phrase best describes each example.

1. **a.** fast   slow
   b. fast   slow

2. **a.** loud   soft
   b. loud   soft

3. **a.** getting faster   getting slower
   b. getting faster   getting slower

Perform, Create

What You Can Do

Sing the Blues

Sing "Good Mornin', Blues." Create a new verse in ⓐ ⓐ ⓑ form.

Play Rhythms

Tap each of the following rhythms four times in the palm of your hand.

a.

b.

c.

Choose an instrument and play the same rhythms again along with the recording of *"Ayelivi."*

Create a Rhythm

Compose a new 8-beat rhythm pattern using , and . Play your pattern for the class.

Let's Get Steppin'!

Move with energy. Show the strong beats.

CD 3–19

Step in Time

Words and Music by Richard M. and Robert B. Sherman

1. Kick your knees up, step in time!
2. Spin a - bout and step in time!

Kick your knees up, step in time!
Spin a - bout and step in time!

Nev - er need a rea - son, nev - er need a rhyme,
Nev - er need a rea - son, nev - er need a rhyme,

Kick your knees up, step in time!
Spin a - bout and step in time!

3. Link your elbows, step in time! . . .
4. 'Round the circle, step in time! . . .

5. Flap like a birdie, step in time! . . .
6. Step in time, step in time! . . .

74

Learning the Language of MUSIC

Ragtime Beats

Ragtime is a style of music with strong beats in unexpected places. **Listen** to this ragtime piano piece. **Move** to show the stronger beats.

CD 3–21
The Entertainer

by Scott Joplin

Scott Joplin was the most famous composer of ragtime music. The U.S. Postal Service even put Joplin's picture on a postage stamp!

Accents!

Say this poem in rhythm. Add **accents** to give it some pizzazz.

An **accent** gives extra importance to a note in a rhythm pattern.

An **accent** on a note looks like this.

CD 3–22

Boogie Chant and Dance

Street Rhyme

Ladies and gentlemen and children too,
These dancin' kids gonna boogie for you.
They're gonna turn all around,
They're gonna touch the ground,
They're gonna shake their shoulders
Till the sun goes down.
Hands up! Ha-ha, Ha-ha-ha!
Hands down! Ha-ha, Ha-ha-ha!
Got a penny, call Jack Benny. Ha-ha, Ha-ha-ha!
Got a nickel, buy a pickle. Ha-ha, Ha-ha-ha!
Got a dime, life is fine. Ha-ha, Ha-ha-ha!

Arts Connection

▲ *Modern Painting with Clef* by Roy Lichtenstein, 1967. Artists use accents too. How does the artist use color to create accents in this painting?

Perform with Accents

Find the notes that have accents in "Two Little Sausages." **Move** to show the accents as you listen to the recording.

Then say the rhyme with accents on the right words.

CD 3–24

Two Little Sausages

Traditional Jump-Rope Rhyme

Two lit-tle sau-sag-es fry-ing in a pan,

One went POP! and the oth-er went BLAM!

Hear a New Rhythm

Listen to "Tideo" and **move** to the beat. Do you hear a new rhythm in the song that is not ♩, ♫, or 𝄽? Which words have the new rhythm?

CD 3–26

Tideo

Play-Party Song from Texas

Pass one win-dow Ti - de - o,   Pass two win-dows Ti - de - o,

Pass three win-dows Ti - de - o,   Jin-gle at the win-dow Ti - de - o.

Ti - de - o,   Ti - de - o,   Jin-gle at the win-dow Ti - de - o.

See a New Rhythm

Tap the rhythms in each window as you sing the last part of "Tideo." How many sounds does the new rhythm have?

Jin-gle at the   win-dow   Ti - de   -   o

A "Tideo" Play-Party!

Form two circles, and get ready to **sing** and **move** to "Tideo."

That Rhythm Again

Pat the steady beat as you listen to the song.
Then **tap** the rhythm of the words.

Amarillo Armadillo

CD 3–33

Words and Music by Robert Demmert

Am - a - ril - lo   Ar - ma - dil - lo, that's some   shell!
Am - a - ril - lo   Ar - ma - dil - lo,   ar - mored back.

Still   you   move   a - round   quite   well.
Grab   some   grubs   and   have   a   snack.

Sing that Rhythm

This song has the new rhythm ♩ ♪♪♪♪.
The new rhythm has four sounds and lasts one
beat. Find the rhythm in the song. Then **sing** the
song with rhythm syllables.

Say That Rhythm

Here's a rhyme that also has the new rhythm.
Say the rhyme as you **clap** a steady beat.
Which word does not have the new rhythm?

Jelly in a Dish

CD 3–38

Traditional Jump-Rope Rhyme

Jel - ly   in   a   dish,   Jel - ly   in   a   dish,

Wig - gle wag - gle, wig - gle wag - gle, Jel - ly   in   a   dish!

Groups of Two Beats

The rhythm of "Jelly in a Dish" moves in groups of two beats. Each group of two beats forms a **measure.** Measures are separated by **bar lines.**

A **bar line** is a vertical line drawn through a staff to separate measures.

A **measure** is a grouping of beats separated by bar lines.

bar line

measure

How many measures are in "Jelly in a Dish"?

Hear That Rhythm

Listen to this selection from a symphony by Franz Joseph Haydn. Count how many times you hear .

CD 3–40

Symphony in G, No. 88

Movement 4
by Franz Joseph Haydn

This symphony was composed in 1787, more than 200 years ago.

M·U·S·I·C M·A·K·E·R·S

Franz Joseph Haydn

Franz Joseph Haydn (1732–1809) composed more than 104 symphonies, more than any other composer! He was born in Austria and he was one of twelve children. When he was eight years old, he was sent to Vienna to be a choirboy. There he continued his musical training.

Show What You Know!

Here are three rhythm patterns from the beginnings of songs you know. **Clap** and say each rhythm. Name the songs.

 CD-ROM Create your own rhythm pattern using ♩♩♩♩ with music notation software.

Takes TWO to CRAWFISH

Boogie like a crawfish as you **listen** to this Cajun dance song. **Move** your arms back and forth as you take sliding steps backward.

CD 3–41

Crawfish!

Words and Music by Papillion

VERSE

1. Now there's a funny little dance the Cajun people love to do,
   That when you hear me talk about, you're gonna want to do it too.
   First you shake your little tail, shimmy back a step or two.
   Then put your hands in the air, do like the crawfish do.
   Refrain

2. (Instrumental Verse)
   Refrain

REFRAIN

Craw-fish! Got to do a lit-tle mud bug boo-gie,

Craw-fish! do the mud bug jit-ter-bug boo-gie, Craw-fish!

Do the Mud Bug Boogie

Sing "Crawfish!" and **move** with your partner. Count in your head as you **move**, 1-2, 1-2, 1-2.

Tune In

Some Cajun people fish for crawfish in a bayou. A bayou is a swampy creek.

M·U·S·I·C M·A·K·E·R·S
Papillion

Papillion (born 1957) grew up in Louisiana. His PaPère (grandfather) nicknamed him Papillion, which means "butterfly" in Cajun French, because he loved to dance and wave his arms about whenever he heard Cajun music. Papillion composed "Crawfish!" and other Cajun songs and dance tunes so that children can find a "butterfly" in their own hearts.

What's the FORM?

Sing this old folk song from Germany.
Find the **a** and **b** parts in the song.

CD 3–43

Ein Männlein steht im Walde
(A Little Man in the Woods)

German Words by Hoffmann Von Fallersleben
English Words by Bryan Louiselle

Folk Song from Germany

Ein Männ-lein steht im Wal - de ganz still und stumm;
A lit - tle fel - low stands in the woods a - head.

es hat von lau - ter Pur - pur ein Mänt - lein um.
He wears a pur - ple coat with a hint of red.

Sagt, wer mag das Männ-lein sein, das da steht im Wald al - lein
Tell me who this man can be, stand - ing there so pa - tient - ly,

mit dem pur - pur - ro - ten___ Män - te - lein?
Stand - ing all a - lone in the woods a - head?

Name Your Pattern

Which pattern below matches the form of the song?

1. **a b a b**   2. **a a b b**   3. **a a b a**

Into the Woods

"Ein Männlein steht im Walde" is also part of the opera *Hänsel und Gretel.* **Listen** to the song as it is sung in the opera. What is the form of the song?

CD 3–47

Ein Männlein steht im Walde

from *Hänsel und Gretel*
by Engelbert Humperdinck

In the opera, Gretel sings this folk song when she and Hänsel go to the forest to pick berries.

▲ Hänsel and Gretel from the opera

Water Melodies

A spring is flowing water that comes up out of the ground. **Listen** to how the melody of this song moves like a spring.

CD 3–48

Allá en la fuente
(There at the Spring)

English Words by Luis Eliezar

Folk Song from Mexico

A - llá en la fuen - te ha - bía un cho - rri - to;
A lit - tle spring, feel - ing ver - y fick - le,

se ha - cía gran - do - te, se ha - cía chi - qui - to;
be - gan a flood, then be - came a trick - le.

es - ta - ba de mal hu - mor, po - bre cho - rri - to te - nía ca - lor.
Too much, and then not e - nough, poor lit - tle spring must be in a huff.

▼ Chicago, Illinois

Las Colinas, Texas ▲

Fountain Music

A spring is like a natural fountain. Many cities and villages around the world have fountains. Sometimes fountains inspire composers to write music.

Listen to this music by Respighi [ruh-SPEE-gee]. Use scarves and **move** to show how the music sounds like fountains.

▲ Paris, France

 CD 3–52

La fontana di Trevi al meriggio

from *Fontane di Roma* **(Fountains of Rome) by Ottorino Respighi**

Respighi composed this music to celebrate the beauty of the Trevi Fountain in Rome, Italy.

▼ Trevi Fountain, Rome, Italy

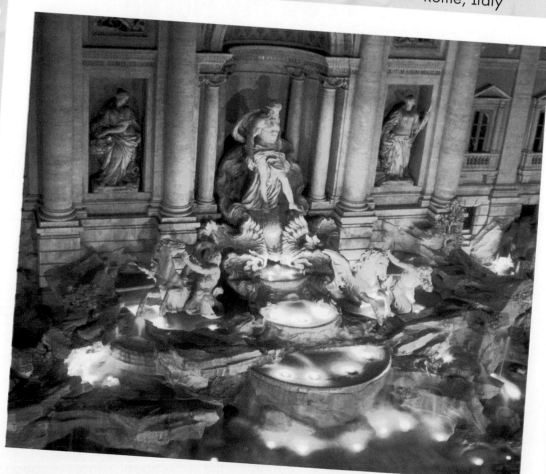

Finding Patterns in Two Songs

Sing a silly song from the Appalachian Mountains. What is unusual about this horse?

CD 4–1

I Fed My Horse

Folk Song from North Carolina

VERSE

1. I fed my horse in a pop-lar trough,

And there he caught the whoop-ing cough.

I fed my horse in a pop-lar trough,

And there he caught the whoop-ing cough.

A Short Pattern

Point to the pitches in the color box as you **sing**. Notice the pattern of the notes. Are they moving upward or downward? How many pitches are there?

REFRAIN

Coy ma lin dow kil ko kil ko,

Coy ma lin dow kil ko me.

2. I fed my horse in a silver spoon,
   And then he kicked it over the moon. *(Repeat)*
   Refrain

3. My old horse is dead and gone,
   But he left his jawbones ploughing the corn. *(Repeat)*
   Refrain

A Latin American Singing Game

Sing a song of friendship. Learn to play a game.

 CD 4–3

Naranja dulce
(Sweet Orange)

English Words by Eva Laurinda

Latin American Singing Game (Mexico and Costa Rica)

1. Na - ran - ja dul - ce, li - món par - ti - do,
1. Sweet hon - ey or - ange, a slice of le - mon,

da - me un a - bra - zo que yo te pi - do.
give me a hug now, my friend I'll miss you.

2. *Si fueran falsos mis juramentos,*
   en otros tiempos se olvidaran.

2. It's time to shake hands, true friends are faithful,
   I'll not forget you, I wish you well.

3. *Toca la marcha, mi pecho llora,*
   adiós señora, yo ya me voy.

3. The march is playing, it's time to go now,
   Goodbye my dear friend, I'm sad to leave you.

Tune In

Children all over the world like to play singing games. "Miss Mary Mack," a hand-clapping game, and "Tideo," a play-party, are popular singing games from the United States.

Compare These Patterns

Melodies are made up of patterns.

Sometimes those patterns repeat.

Sometimes those patterns change.

Sometimes you can find the same pattern in different songs.

Look at these patterns from "I Fed My Horse" and "*Naranja dulce.*"

Compare these patterns.

How are they the same?

How are they different?

Read a NEW PITCH

Listen for the new pitch in this folk song.

CD 4–7

Rocky Mountain

Folk Song from the Southern United States

VERSE

1. Rock - y moun-tain, rock - y moun-tain, rock - y moun-tain high;

When you're on that rock - y moun-tain, hang your head and cry!

REFRAIN

Do, do, do, do, Do re - mem - ber me;

Do, do, do, do, Do re - mem - ber me.

2. Sunny valley, sunny valley,
   sunny valley low;
   When you're in that sunny valley,
   Sing it soft and slow. *Refrain*

3. Stormy ocean, stormy ocean,
   stormy ocean wide;
   When you're on that deep blue sea,
   There's no place you can hide. *Refrain*

Name the Pitch

The new pitch is between *mi* and *do*.
It is called *re*.

mi   re   do

The hand sign for
re looks like this. ▶

Singing with *re*

Now **sing** "Rocky Mountain." When you get to
the refrain, use hand signs and pitch syllables.

Tune In

"Rocky Mountain" is from the
southern United States. One of the main
mountain ranges in this area is the Blue
Ridge Mountains, pictured here.

Sounds of the Sea

Have you ever listened to a sea shell? What did you hear? **Sing** "Sea Shell" and use hand signs.

 CD 4–12

Sea Shell

Words and Music by Pierre Perron

Sea   Shell   Sea   Shell,

Sing   a   song   for   me.

Sing   a - bout   the   o - cean,

Sing   a - bout   the   sea.

New Home for *Do*

In the song "Sea Shell," *do* is in the first space of the staff. Look at the music below. Where is *do* now? Where is *so*?

This time *do* should be on a line, but there are not enough lines on the staff. You can add an extra line for *do* called a **ledger line.**

A **ledger line** is an extra line used for pitches above or below the staff.

ledger line

Show What You Know!

Each melody below comes from a song you know that has *re* in it. Find *do* in each example. Then **sing** each melody with pitch syllables and name the tune.

Colorful

Listen to this song. It is from Nigeria, a country in Africa. **Describe** the timbres of the **percussion** instruments that you hear.

Percussion instruments are played by shaking, scraping, or striking.

CD 4–17

Ise oluwa

Yoruba Folk Song from Nigeria

do

I - se ___ o - lu - wa ___ ko le ba - je - oh; ___

I - se ___ o - lu - wa ___ ko le ba - je - oh. ___

Ko le ba - je - oh, ___ ko le ba - je - oh. ___

I - se ___ o - lu - wa ___ ko le ba - je - oh; ___

I - se ___ o - lu - wa ___ ko le ba - je - oh. ___

Sounds

Be an African Drummer!

Play these patterns with
"Ise oluwa."

↓	↑	↑	↓	↑	↑
•			•		
Low		High	Low		High

Listen to the *balafons* [BAH-lah-fohns]
on the recording. These are percussion
instruments from West Africa.
Describe the timbre.

CD 4–20
Nangapè

by Yaya Diallo

The *balafon* is a type of xylophone made from
bamboo and gourds. The keys are made of
bamboo reeds. Gourds are hollowed out and
hung underneath each key to amplify the sound.

Percussion from Bali

The *gamelan* is a set of instruments from Bali. It includes percussion. **Listen** to this recording to learn how the *kendang,* the *gong,* the *gangsa,* and the *kempli* sound.

CD 4–21

Gamelan Montage

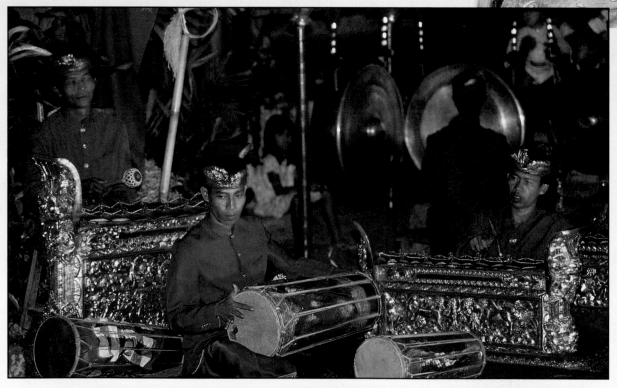

▲ *Gamelan*

How many percussion instruments do you see? What are they made of?

 Video Library Watch *Percussion Instruments: Tuned* to see and hear an example of *gamelan.*

Gamelan Game

Listen to the way instruments weave their sounds together in *Ujan mas*. Point to the instruments as you hear them in the recording.

CD 4–22

Ujan mas

by Gde Purana

Ujan mas means "golden rain" in Balinese.

Ujan mas Listening Map

Gangsa

Gong

Kendang

Kempli

Creating Textures

What do you do while waiting for a traffic light to change? You can **sing** this song as you wait.

Play these ostinatos with the song to create a thicker texture.

Playing Lullaby Layers

Sing this lullaby from Africa. Abiyoyo is a character in South African folk stories.

CD 4–25

ABIYOYO

Bantu Lullaby

do–

G   C

A - bi - yo - yo, _____ a - bi - yo - yo, _____

G   C

A - bi - yo - yo, _____ a - bi - yo - yo;

Am   F   C

A - bi - yo - yo, bi - yo - yo, bi - yo - yo, _____

Am   F   C

A - bi - yo - yo, bi - yo - yo, bi - yo - yo. _____

Building Music Layers

Play these patterns with the song. Each pattern adds a new layer of sound.

Describe how adding the layers changes the texture of the music. Does the texture become thinner or thicker?

Alto Xylophone

Bass Xylophone

▼ Many African lullabies are about scary monsters like Abiyoyo.

Review, Assess,

What Do You Know?

1. Look at the rhythm of "Amarillo Armadillo" on page 82. Find and point to the following rhythms.

   a. ♫   **b.** ♩   **c.** ♬♬

2. Look at "Amarillo Armadillo" again.

   a. Find and point to the barlines.
   b. How many measures are in the song?

3. Read the pitches in *"Naranja dulce"* on page 96. How many times does each of these pitches occur in the song?

   a. *so*   **b.** *la*   **c.** *mi*   **d.** *re*   **e.** *do*

What Do You Hear? 3

 CD 4–27

Listen to the four rhythm patterns on the recording. Match the patterns you hear with the rhythms below.

Perform, Create

What You Can Do

Move with an Accent

Move to show the accented and unaccented beats in "Crawfish!" Perform larger movements for accented beats. Perform smaller movements for unaccented beats.

Perform Rhythms

As you listen to the recording of "Amarillo Armadillo," pat each of these rhythm patterns.

a.

b.

Create a Melody

Create a melody for "Jelly in a Dish." Use only these pitches.

do re mi so la do re mi so la
C   D   E   G   A   C   D   E   G   A

Have your melody end on *do*. Perform your melody on a xylophone or metallophone.

Samba!

In the 1930s, Carmen Miranda came to the United States from Brazil. She brought with her the *samba* style of music. **Listen** to *Chica chica boom chic* and **move** to the music.

CD 4–31
Chica chica boom chic
by Mack Gordon and Harry Warren

In this song, Miranda expresses her pride in being Brazilian.

Here is a *samba* rhythm you can **play** along with the recording.

M·U·S·I·C M·A·K·E·R·S

Carmen Miranda

Carmen Miranda (1909–1955) was famous as the Banana Lady. She appeared in TV commercials and advertisements for bananas. She was known for her "tutti-frutti" hat. Miranda became a singing, dancing movie star in Hollywood.

Building Our Musical Skills

Going Bananas

Here is a song about bananas you can **sing**.

CD 4–32

Banana

REFRAIN
All

Words and Music by Flor De Caña

C   G7

All   the na - tions like ba - na - na. _____

G7   C   Fine

All   the rac - es like ba - na - na. __

Expressing the

How do storms make you feel? How does the child in the song feel about this tropical storm?

Listen to *"La tormenta tropical."* When the song gets gradually louder, this is called a **crescendo.** Find the crescendos in the music.

A **crescendo** (————) occurs when the music gets gradually louder.

CD 4–34
MIDI 8

La tormenta tropical
(The Tropical Storm)

Words and Music by Juanita Newland Ulloa

VERSE

1. *Despierta, hija, despierta,*
   es hora de levantar.
   No importa si hay sol o lluvia,
   es hora de estudiar.
   Refrain

2. *Entonces cierro las ventanas*
   el viento soplará.
   El cielo estara enojado
   y pronto llorará.
   Refrain

3. *Por fin sale el sol.*
   El viento se calló.
   las gotas se apagan
   la lluvia se paró.
   Refrain

1. Wake up, wake up, oh my dear one.
   Wake up and start a new day.
   No matter if there's sun or raindrops,
   We've much to do on this day.
   Refrain

2. We'll stay inside while it's raining.
   Let's get the windows shut tight.
   The sky is getting dark like it's nighttime!
   Sit here with me 'til it's light.
   Refrain

3. We'll listen to the storm raging.
   Glad we're inside on this day.
   Tomorrow we'll go out and see puddles,
   When the dark clouds all go away.
   Refrain

Weather

REFRAIN

Ay   ma - mi, no quier - o   des - per - tar - me.
Oh,   please, mom - my, I   don't want to   wake   up.

Al - go pa - sa, lo ___ sien - to   ya. ___
I   can see   that storm _ clouds are   here. _

Es que vie - ne, vie - ne la tor - men - ta,
I   can feel   that some - thing is ___ com - ing.

la tor - men - ta trop - i - cal. ___
Now the tropi - cal storm _ is   near. ___

A Weather Proverb

A proverb is a wise old saying.
Say this proverb about weather.

"Whether it's cold or whether it's hot,
We shall have weather, whether or not."

Decide which words to say loudly or softly.
Which words might get accents? Where can
you make a *crescendo*?

Creating with Expression

- **Compose** a melody for the proverb using
  only these pitches.

- Teach your melody to a partner.

- **Perform** your melody with dynamics.

Listening for Expression

Listen to *Saudação*. How does the listening map show changes in the dynamics? What parts of the map show loud or soft?

CD 4–38

Saudação

from *Concerto for Marimba and String Orchestra* by Ney Rosauro

Rosauro is a composer from Brazil. He writes music for marimba and other percussion.

Saudação
Listening Map

f Introduction *p*   Main Theme *mf*   Main Theme *f*

2
(0:22)

p
(0:47)   Main Theme *f*   Main Theme *ff*

3

f   4a   4b   *ff*

(0:59)   (1:03)

5

Banjo Rhythms

What instrument does Dinah play in the song?
Now **sing** "Dinah."

CD 4–39

Dinah

Folk Song from the United States

No one's in the house but Di - nah, Di - nah,

No one's in the house but me, I know.

No one's in the house but Di - nah, Di - nah,

Strum - min' on the old ban - jo.

Sing Your Name

Sing the song again. Sing your name and
the name of an instrument you'd like to play!

Dinah's Got Rhythm!

The rhythms in each house equal one beat. **Listen** to "Dinah" again. Can you find each rhythm in the song?

You've Got Rhythm!

Clap and say the rhythm in each house. Then put the houses in any order to **compose** your own rhythm piece. **Perform** it on an instrument.

Arts Connection

◀ *The Banjo Lesson* by Mary Cassatt (1845–1926)

Cooking with Rhythm

Sing this song and **move** the way the words tell you!

Old Brass Wagon

CD 4-44

Play-Party from the United States

1. Cir - cle to the left, old brass wag - on;
2. Cir - cle to the right, old brass wag - on;

Cir - cle to the left, old brass wag - on;
Cir - cle to the right, old brass wag - on;

Cir - cle to the left, old brass wag - on;
Cir - cle to the right, old brass wag - on;

You're the one, my dar - lin'.
You're the one, my dar - lin'.

3. Swing, oh, swing, . . .

4. Promenade right, . . .

5. Walk it up and down, . . .

6. Break and swing, . . .

Rhythm Stew

Look for this rhythm pattern
in "Old Brass Wagon."

How many times did
you find it?

Create a rhythm piece with
these rhythms.

Play your piece on fun
instruments. Try some spoons.

Show What You Know!

These rhythm patterns are from songs you know. What
words go with them? Name and **sing** the songs they
came from.

1. $\frac{2}{4}$

2. $\frac{2}{4}$

A Longer Sound

Listen to "*Frère Jacques.*" **Tap** the steady beat. Which sounds last for more than one beat? Find them on this chart.

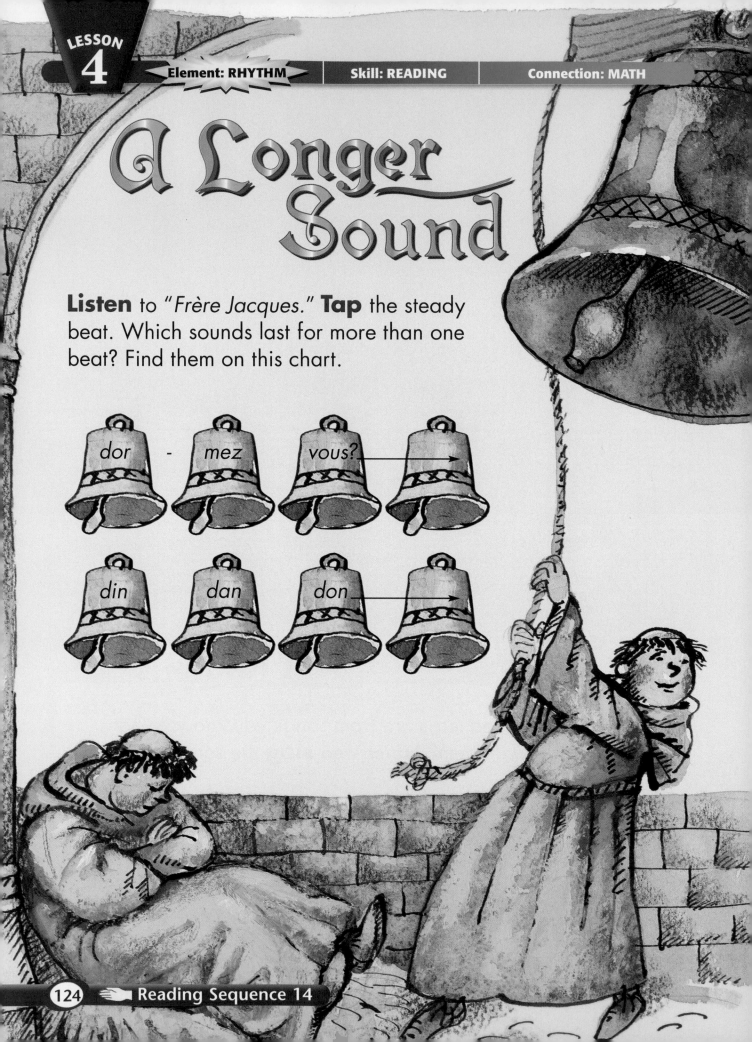

dor - mez   vous?   →

din   dan   don   →

One + One = ?

Some sounds in *"Frère Jacques"* last more than one beat.

♩ = 1 beat

♩ + ♩ = 2 beats

You can use a **tie** to join the two notes together.

♩‿♩ = 2 beats

tie

A **tie** is a musical symbol that joins two notes together to create a longer sound.

Find the ties in the music.
Then **sing** the song in French and English.

CD 5–1

Frère Jacques
(Are You Sleeping?)

Folk Song from France

Frè - re   Jac - ques,   Frè - re   Jac - ques,
Are   you   sleep - ing,   Are   you   sleep - ing,

Dor - mez   vous? ____   Dor - mez   vous? ____
Broth - er   John, ____   Broth - er   John? ____

Son - nez les ma - ti - nes,   Son - nez les ma - ti - nes,
Morn-ing bells are ring - ing,   Morn-ing bells are ring - ing,

Din,   dan,   don, ____   din,   dan,   don.
Ding,   dang,   dong, ____   ding,   dang,   dong. ____

Phrases That Move You!

A **phrase** is a part of a melody.
The melody of this song has four phrases.
Listen to hear how each phrase ends.

A **phrase** is a
musical sentence.

CD 5–8 **A Song That's Just for You**

Words and Music by Bryan Louiselle

It may be high   or low,   It may be fast   or slow,

It   may   be short   or   long. __

It could be rap   or rock,   It could be bop   or Bach,

It   could be   soft   or   strong. _

Play Phrase Statues

Play a statue game with your classmates.
Stand in a circle. At the end of each phrase,
jump into the center and pose like a statue.

It does-n't mat-ter what the tune __ is,

or if the style is old __ or new; __

If you en-joy the sound, it means you might have found __

a song that's just for you. __

Miles of Melody

Long ago, English children sang this song. They pretended they could travel all the way to Babylon in just one day. **Sing** the song and **play** the game.

CD 5–10

How Many Miles to Babylon?

Game Song from England

How ma-ny miles to Ba-by-lon? Three score and ten.

Will we be there by can-dle-light? Yes, and back a-gain.

O-pen the gates and let us through. Not with-out a beck and bow.

Here's your beck; here's your bow! O-pen the gates and let us through.

Miles to Go for *mi-re-do!*

Find the places in the song with *mi*, *re*, and *do* only. **Sing** those places with pitch syllables.

"Here's your beck"

"Here's your bow"

"Open the gates and let us through"

Tune In

Babylon was once a city near present-day Baghdad, Iraq.

Grow a Melody

The melody for this song was written by children from Upper Nyack, New York. The words are from a proverb, or wise old saying.

CD 5–17

Plant Four Seeds

Southern Proverb

Music by Students from Upper Nyack, NY

Plant four seeds when you make a row,

One to rot and one to grow,

One for the pig-eon and one for the crow.

Play these patterns with the song.

Bass Xylophone   Xylophone

Create a Sound Garden

Compose a melody to add a new section to "Plant Four Seeds." Use names of flowers and vegetables you might plant in your garden. Here is an example.

Xylophone

Ru - ta - ba - ga, squash,   ros - es,   dai - sy.

Use only these pitches in your melody.

C D E   G A   C D E   G A

A Melody Without Words

Listen to the way this composer created a melody with these pitches.

CD 5–19
Allegretto

by Gunild Keetman

On this recording you will hear xylophones, maracas, tambourine, and tom-toms.

A Flood of Sound

Listen for the rhythm in this speech piece. When you hear it, shuffle your feet in that rhythm.

CD 5–20

Mississippi River Chant

by Bill Martin Jr.

Mississippi River morning Mississippi **sun,**
Mississippi River warning thunder wonder **done.**
Mississippi River raining Mississippi **flood,**
Mississippi River waning oozy newsy **mud.**
Shuffle to the **left** shuffle to the **left,**
shuffle shuffle shuffle shuffle,
shuffle to the **left.**
Mississippi River morning Mississippi **sun,**
Mississippi River warning thunder wonder **done.**

Mississippi Melody

Play rhythms from the speech piece on a xylophone. Use only these pitches.

Mississippi Rhythm

Now **compose** an ostinato with words from the speech piece. **Play** it on one of these instruments.

A Five-Pitch Song

In Korea a bell rings to start the school day. How does your school day begin? **Listen** to this Korean school song. Which words sound like a bell?

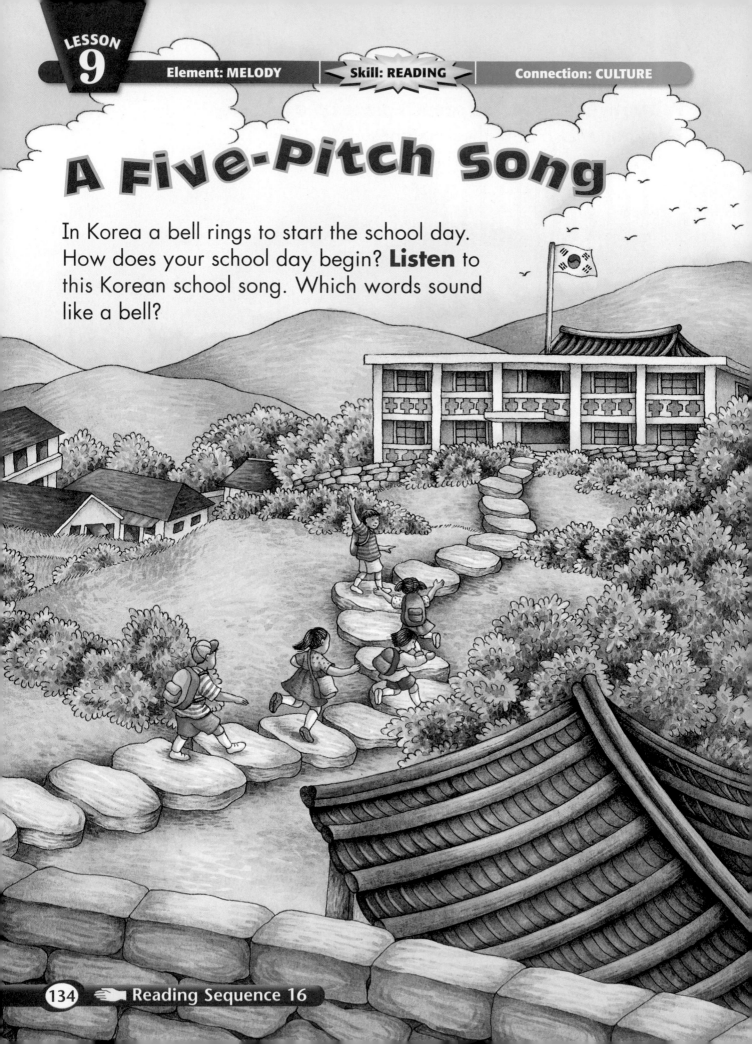

Five Familiar Pitches

"Ha'kyo jong" has five pitches that you already know. **Listen** to the song again. What pitch ends the song? Hint: The song starts on *so*.

CD 5–22

Ha'kyo jong

(School Bell Sounding)

School Song from Korea
English Words by David Eddleman   *Words and Music by Mary Kimm Joh*

1. Ha' - kyo   jong   ee   daeng   daeng   daeng,
1. School bell sound - ing,   ding,   dong,   ding,

Uh - sə   mo   ee   jha,
Let   us   gath - er   in.

Sun   saeng   nim   ee   oo   ree   rul,
Greet   the   teach - er   by   the   door,

Ki - da   ree   shin   da.
Let   the   class   be - gin.

2. Ha'kyo jong ee daeng daeng daeng,
   Uhsə mo ee jha,
   Sa ee joht keh oh nuhldoh,
   Khong bu jhal ha jha.

2. School bell sounding, ding, dong, ding,
   Let us gather in.
   Working all together now,
   Learning once again.

Sing a Pentatonic Song

When a song ends on *do* and has only four other pitches, it is called *do* **pentatonic.** Now **sing** *"Ha'kyo jong"* with pitch syllables and hand signs.

Songs that have only five pitches are sometimes called **pentatonic**.

Play Along with the Song

Here are some patterns you can **play** as the class sings *"Ha'kyo jong."*

Hearing Pentatonic

Listen to *Arirang*, a well-known folk song from Korea. Each section ends on *do*. Raise your hand when you hear *do* in the recording.

CD 5–29

Arirang

Traditional from Korea
as performed by the Dieter Ilg Trio
This traditional melody is performed here by a jazz group.

Show What You Know!

Each of these melodies comes from a song you may know. **Sing** each one with pitch syllables and hand signs.

1. do mi so la mi mi re re do

2. do so do so mi mi re re do

3. mi mi mi mi so so so so la so mi

String Sounds

Some string instruments are played with a bow. Some are plucked, and some are struck like percussion.

Listen to these string players perform a lively dance tune. **Describe** the different timbres you hear.

Tune In

String instruments make sound because their strings vibrate.

▼ hammered dulcimer

▼ string bass

More String Sounds

See and hear more examples of string instruments by going to the Sound Bank on page 420. Find the viola, cello, banjo, guitar, and the mountain dulcimer. How are they the same or different from the instruments in *Cold and Frosty Morning*?

CD 5–30

Cold and Frosty Morning

Traditional English Country Dance Tune

Some of the instruments on this recording are Celtic harp, string bass, hammered dulcimer, and fiddle.

▼ Celtic harp

fiddle (violin) ▶

Electric Strings

Some string players change the way their instruments sound by attaching an electronic "pickup." The "pickup" sends the sound to other electronic equipment which changes the sound.

▼ pickup

▼ amplifier

▲ "wah" pedal

An Electric Fiddle

Listen to Eileen Ivers play her electric blue fiddle. *Fiddle* is another name for the violin. Notice when the fiddle sounds "normal" and when it sounds very different. **Describe** what you hear.

 CD 5–31
Riverdance Suite

by John Whelan

This piece is an arrangement of some of the music from the dance show *Riverdance*.

M·U·S·I·C M·A·K·E·R·S

Eileen Ivers

Eileen Ivers (born 1965) is one of the top fiddle players in the world today. She was born in New York City and spent much of her childhood in both New York and Ireland. Ivers won her first award for fiddle playing when she was nine years old. She is most famous for playing fiddle in the show *Riverdance*.

Turkish Textures

Sing this folk song from Turkey, a country in the Middle East.

 CD 5–32

Adana ya gidelim
(Let's Go to Adana)

English Words by C. P. Language Institute   *Folk Song from Turkey*

A - da - na _____ ya _____ gi - de - lim.
Let's   go   to   A - da - na and eat or - an - ges.

Por - ta - kal - lar - i _____ yi - ye - lim.
There _ they _ have the sweet - est __ or - an - ges.

Play this pattern with the song. It will sound good as an **accompaniment.**

> An **accompaniment** is music that is performed with a melody.

Xylophone

142

Texture Time!

Say and **play** the words *Let's go to Adana* on a hand drum.

Let's go to A - da - na.

Create a thicker texture by playing this ostinato on a wood block.

A - da - na

Play finger cymbals to give a little "zing" to the texture.

Video Library Describe the texture of the music you hear in *Performing in Groups*.

Music Among

A long time ago, stars helped sailors find their way around the oceans.

Sing this starry song.

CD 5–38

Oh, Watch the Stars

Folk Song from South Carolina

Oh, watch the stars, see how they run.

Oh, watch the stars, see how they run. _____

The _ stars run down _____ at the set-ting of the sun.

Oh, watch the stars, see how they run.

the Stars

Playing Among the Stars

Now **play** this ostinato with the song. Which hand moves right and left?

Alto metallophone

Alto metallophone

Compose other "twinkly" sounds to add to your starry texture. Describe how the artist shows stars in the painting.

Arts Connection

▼ *Starry Night, 1923–1924* by Edvard Munch

Review, Assess,

What Do You Know?

Read the melodies below. Then find and point to all the pitches called *re*. How many did you find in each?

a.

b.

What Do You Hear? 4A

CD 5–41

You will hear three musical examples. Each example has two phrases. Decide if the phrases in each example are the same or different.

1. same   different
2. same   different
3. same   different

What Do You Hear? 4B

CD 5–44

Listen to these string instruments. Decide how each is being played.

1. bowed   plucked   struck
2. bowed   plucked   struck
3. bowed   plucked   struck

Perform, Create

What You Can Do

Perform Rhythms

Pat each of these rhythm patterns. Then say the rhythms, using syllables.

a.

b.

c.

Create a Rhythm Piece

Create an eight-measure percussion piece, using the three patterns above. Decide which pattern will come first, second, third, and fourth. Add dynamic markings to make your piece more expressive and interesting. Use *forte*, *piano*, and *crescendo*. Perform your piece for the class on an unpitched instrument of your choice.

Ways to Explore

If you could not see, how would you learn about the world? Close your eyes and learn through your ears and hands.

Sing this song that expresses how much you can learn through touch.

CD 5–47

I See with My Hands

Words and Music by Marcy Marxer

VERSE

1. I see with my hands   The clouds, the sky, the land;

The fish that swim in the deep blue sea,

The sun that shines on you and me.   I see with my hands.

REFRAIN

See, _____   see, _____

ev - 'ry cur - i - os - i - ty; ___

Discovering New Musical Horizons

See, _____ see, _____

D. C.
Last time to Coda

in my hands I hold the key. ____

Coda (after verse 3 only)

(Repeat 2 times)

I see with ___ my hands.

2. I see with my hands
   The clouds, the sky, the land;
   A bird, a flow'r, a warm embrace,
   And my best friend's smiling face.
   I see with my hands. *Refrain*

3. I see with my hands
   The clouds, the sky, the land;
   A stone, a stream, a melody,
   The people in my family.
   I see with my hands. *Refrain*

Listening to Learn

Follow the map as you **listen** to *Fanfarre*.
Compare the dynamics of the guitars with the
other instruments. How are they different?

CD 5–49

Fanfarre (Allegro Marziale)

**from *Concierto Madrigal for Two Guitars and Orchestra*
by Joaquín Rodrigo**

Rodrigo composed this piece especially for the guitarists
perfoming on this recording, the Romeros.

 Listening Map

MUSIC MAKERS

Joaquín Rodrigo

Joaquín Rodrigo (1901–1999), born in Spain, was blind from age three due to illness. He started studying music at a young age and won many awards for his compositions. He was one of Spain's leading composers of the twentieth century.

Connected Sounds— Separated Sounds

A melody can sound smooth and connected. It can also sound short and separated. **Listen** to "Party Tonight!" **Identify** the parts that are **legato** and the parts that are **staccato.**

A **legato** melody has smooth, connected pitches.

A **staccato** melody has short, separated pitches.

CD 5–50

Party Tonight!

Words and Music by Jill Gallina

With a Swing

All the an-i-mals at the zoo ___

are hav-ing a par-ty to-night. ___

Hop-pin' and bop-pin', roll-in' and rock-in',

did you ev-er see such a sight? ___

Moving *Legato*, Moving *Staccato*

Move like the animals. To show *legato*, you can swing your arms and turn around. To show *staccato*, you can use short hops and twists. You can also **create** your own movements.

1. Hip-hop-pin' hip - pos, the grace-ful danc-ing bears,
2. A rock-in' rhin - o, a waltz-ing pea-cock too,

stomp, stomp-in' el - e - phants _ so loud it hurts our ears. _
swing danc-in' mon-keys and _ a twist-in' kan-ga-roo. _

A hy - e - na does the hu - la, oh, what a sight!
There's a bal - let danc-ing zeb - ra, oh, what a sight!

So come on down, _ come on down, _

join our par - ty to - night. __

Listening for *Legato* and *Staccato*

Listen to *Toccata and Tango*. Do the percussion instruments sound *legato* or *staccato*? How do the string instruments sound?

CD 5–52

Toccata and Tango

by David Hanson

The solo percussionist is Steve Houghton. After making this recording he said, ". . . one of life's great pleasures is making music with your friends!"

MUSIC MAKERS
Steve Houghton

Steve Houghton (born 1954) is a percussionist, jazz drummer, composer, and teacher. He performs with symphony orchestras and jazz ensembles. He has spent many years teaching percussion to young people.

A *Legato* and *Staccato* Dance

Create a dance to *Toccata and Tango*. Show *staccato* with short, sudden movements. **Move** smoothly with a flowing scarf to show *legato*.

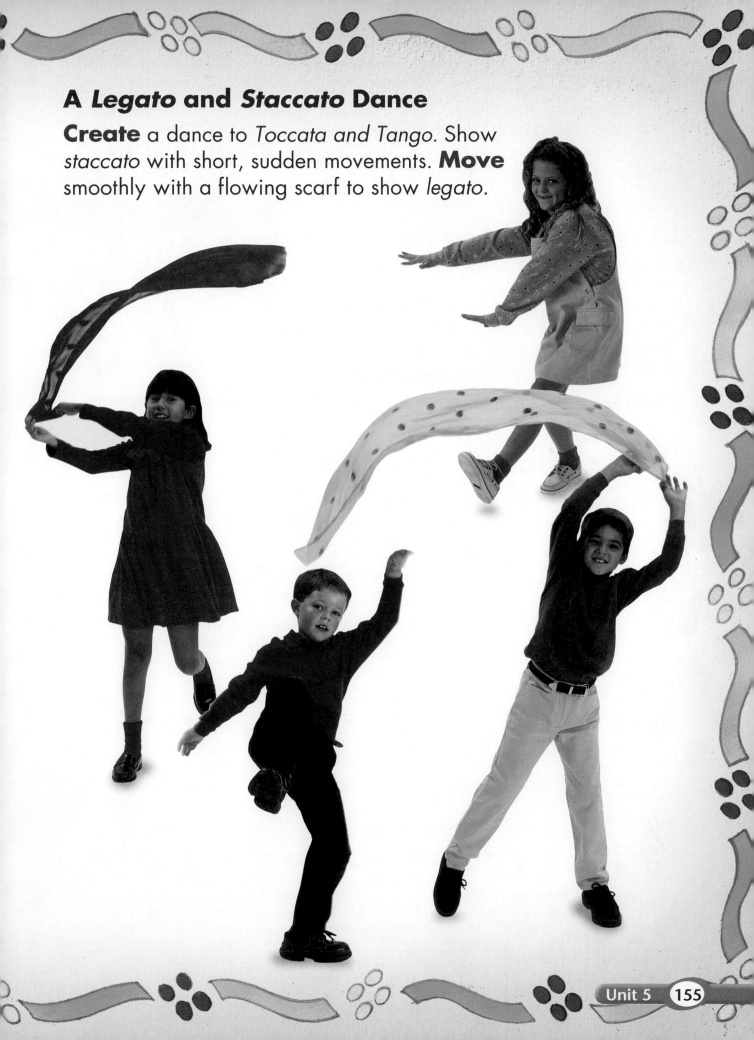

Two Beats Long

Listen to this Spanish song from Costa Rica. Which sounds are longer than the others?

CD 6–1

Mariposita
(Little Butterfly)

English Words by Eva Laurinda   *Words and Music by Wilber Alpírez Quesada*

Lin - da ma - ri - po - sa   que jue - gas fe - liz, ___
Pret - ty but - ter - fly, ___ ⅔   play - ing cheer - ful - ly, ___

en - tre tan - tas flo - res,   en - tre tan - tas ro - sas.
in the flow - er gar - den,   with the man - y ros - es.

Prés - ta - me tus a - las,   tus a - las pre - cio - sas,
Let me try your wings, _ ⅔   pre-cious lit - tle wings _ so

que tam - bién yo quie - ro,   ju - gar con las ro - sas.
I can al - so play _ with   all the pret - ty ros - es.

156

Singing Long Sounds

Now **sing** *"Mariposita."* Make sure that you sing ♩ ♩ for two whole beats.

Two-Beat Moves

Sing the song again. **Move** to show the difference between the shorter and longer sounds.

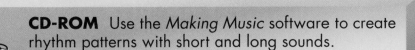

CD-ROM Use the *Making Music* software to create rhythm patterns with short and long sounds.

Two Beats in One

In China the melody of "Hui jia qü" is played as the children line up to go home from school.

CD 6–5

Hui jia qü

(Home from School)

English Words by David Eddleman   Folk Song from China

功　　课___　完　　毕___　要　　回　　家
Gong　ke ___　wan　bi ___　yao　hui　jia
When　the ___　sun　is ___　sink - ing　low,

收　　拾___　书　　包　　回　　家___　去
Shou　shi ___　shu　bao　hui　jia ___　qü
Home - ward __　from　my　school　I ___　go,

看　　见___　父　　母___　行　　个　　礼
Kan　jian ___　fu　mu ___　xing　ge　li
There　where _　I　know _　I　will　find

父　　母___　对　　我___　笑　　嘻　　嘻
Fu　mu __　dui ___　wo ___　xiao　xi　xi.
Wait - ing, ___　fa - ther　and　moth - er　kind.

Read a New Note

Sing *"Hui jia qü"* and **tap** the beat. One of the notes lasts for two beats. It can be written like this: ♩ or like this: ♩♩

Find each ♩ in the song. **Sing** the song again with rhythm syllables.

Play this pattern with the song.

Arts Connection

Jinshan Peasant Painting. Jinshan is a county in China, near Shanghai. This is a painting of children playing in a schoolyard. ▶

Elephant Rhythms

Children in Chile sing this game song. Look for each ♩ in *"Un elefante."* **Sing** the song with rhythm syllables.

CD 6–12

Un elefante

(An Elephant)

Singing Game from Chile

English Words by Alice Firgau

Words and Music by Claudina de Ferrari

1. Un e - le - fan - te se ba - lan - cea - ba
1. There on a cob - web made by a spi - der

so - bre la te - la de u - na a - ra - ña,
Sat a big el - e - phant a - swing - ing,

Co - mo ve - í - a que re - sis - tí - a
Then just to see how strong it could be, he

fue a lla - mar a un ca - ma - ra - da.
called for a friend to come and join him.

Add Instruments

Play these patterns with *"Un elefante."* Imagine the drum is an elephant. Imagine the finger cymbals are the spider weaving its web.

2. *Dos elefantes*
   se balanceaban
   sobre la tela de una araña,
   Como veían que resistía
   fueron a llamar
   a un camarada.

3. *Tres elefantes . . .*
4. *Cuatro elefantes . . .*
5. *Cinco elefantes . . .*
6. *Seis elefantes . . .*
7. *Siete elefantes . . .*
8. *Ocho elefantes . . .*
9. *Nueve elefantes . . .*
10. *Diez elefantes . . .*

2. There on a cobweb
   made by a spider
   Sat two big elephants a-swinging,
   Then just to see how strong it could be,
   They called for a friend
   to come and join them.

3. . . .Sat three big elephants . . .
4. . . .Sat four big elephants . . .
5. . . .Sat five big elephants . . .
6. . . .Sat six big elephants . . .
7. . . .Sat seven big elephants . . .
8. . . .Sat eight big elephants . . .
9. . . .Sat nine big elephants . . .
10. . . .Sat ten big elephants . . .

Tune In

Some tropical spiders live in groups in large webs. They cooperate to build and repair the web.

Baby Elephant Walk

Listening Map

Let's Play an Elephant Song

Play these rhythm patterns with *Baby Elephant Walk* while the rest of the class follows the listening map.

Imagine the drum part is the mother elephant walking. Imagine the wood block is the baby elephant learning to walk.

CD 6–19
Baby Elephant Walk

by Henry Mancini

Show What You Know!

Find the rhythm patterns on the spider webs that add up to two beats. How many beats are in the other spider webs?

Questions and Answers

This song is in question and answer form. A musical question is a phrase that seems to need a musical answer. As you **sing** "Same Train," find the question and answer phrases.

 CD 6–20

Same Train

English Version by Holsaert-Bailey   *African American Folk Melody*

1. Same train _ a - blow - in' at the sta - tion,
2. Same train _ a - com - in' down the line, _

Same train, _ same train. _
Same train, _ same train. _

Same train _ wait - in' for the peo - ple,
Same train _ pick - in' up ___ speed, _

Same train, _ same train. _
Same train, _ same train. _

Same train ___ leav - in' the sta - tion,
Same train ___ go - in' like six - ty,

Same train ___ be back to - mor - row,
Same train ___ be back to - mor - row,

Same train, ___ same train. ___
Same train, ___ same train. ___

3. Same train a-chuggin' up the mountain, ⎫ 2 times
   Hard pull, hard pull,   ⎭
   Same train easy down the mountain,
   Same train be back tomorrow, . . .

4. Same train a-passin' all the farmyards, ⎫ 2 times
   Same train, same train.   ⎭
   Same train a-passin' all the farmyards,
   Same train be back tomorrow, . . .

5. Same train a-whistlin' at the crossroads, ⎫ 2 times
   Same train, same train.   ⎭
   Same train a-whistlin' at the crossroads,
   Same train be back tomorrow, . . .

6. Same train a-comin' to the tunnel, . . .
   Same train a-speedin' through the tunnel, . . .
   Same train out in the sunlight,
   Same train be back tomorrow, . . .

7. Same train a-blowin' for the station, . . .
   Same train a-stoppin' at the station, . . .
   Same train a-droppin' all the people,
   Same train be back tomorrow, . . .

Two Sections, Two Movements

Some songs have more than one section.
Listen to "Sing a Rainbow." What clues
tell you where a new section begins?

A

 CD 6–22

Sing a Rainbow

Words and Music by Arthur Hamilton

Red   and   yel - low   and   pink   and   green,

pur - ple   and   orange   and   blue,

I   can   sing   a   rain - bow,   sing   a   rain - bow,

sing   a   rain - bow,   too.

Rainbow Dance

How would you listen with your eyes?

Create movements for the (A) section of the song.

Move a different way for the (B) section.

Dinosaur Forms

Listen to "Dinosaur Dance." Does this song have **Ⓐ** and **Ⓑ** sections only? There is a new section at the very end of the song with this symbol ⊕. It is called a **coda.**

A **coda** is a short section added to the end of a song.

Words and Music by Ned Ginsburg

CD 6–24
MIDI 9

Dinosaur Dance

VERSE

1. Thousands and thousands
   of years ago,
   dinosaurs ruled the land.
   They plodded through their
   humdrum lives,
   and snow and mud and sand!
   But ev'ry once in a while,
   even dinosaurs need some fun.
   So they'd throw themselves a party
   right out in the scorching sun!
   And to this day,
   we celebrate the dinosaur way:
   Refrain

2. You don't need fancy
   dancin' shoes,
   don't strut your stylish stuff.
   Just do like a
   brontosaurus,
   that's sure to be enough!
   And don't make fun of your neighbor.
   'cause he's liable to chew you out!
   Just join in the jumpin' madness,
   that's what it's all about.
   Now, once again,
   you got to get ready, my friend:
   Refrain

Lift your di-no-saur knee,   wig-gle your di-no-saur toes,

raise your di-no-saur hand,   and touch your di-no-saur nose.

Dinosaur Dancing

Create a dance that shows the difference between the **A** and **B** sections of the song. How will you **move** for the *coda*?

Wag your di-no-saur tail,   now hold your di-no-saur stance.

D. C. Last time to ⊕

Whad-da-ya know?   You're do-in' the di - no-saur dance!

⊕ *Coda*

Whad-da - ya know?   You're do - in' the di - no - saur

dance! __

A MELODY to Sing

"All Around the Buttercup" is a singing game. How many phrases are in the song? As you **sing** the song, notice how the phrases end.

All Around the Buttercup

CD 6–26

Traditional Singing Game from the United States

All a-round the but-ter cup, one, two, three.

If you want a nice young friend, just choose me.

Identify the Pitches

What is the first pitch of "All Around the Buttercup"? What pitch ends the first phrase? What pitch ends the second phrase?

A Game to Play

Playing the Buttercup Game

- Form a circle and hold hands.
- Raise your arms to make "windows."
- The leader moves around the circle, weaving in and out of the windows.

Pentatonic Calypso

"Cookie" is a pentatonic song in the calypso style. **Listen** to the song. **Sing** the responses. Then **sing** the calls.

CD 6–31

Cookie

Calypso Song from the West Indies

Cook-ie, you sure no-bod-y passed here? No, my friend.

Cook-ie, you sure no-bod-y passed here? No, my friend. Well!

One of me dump-lin's gone! Don't tell ___ me so!

One of me dump-lin's gone! Don't tell ___ me so!

One of me dump-lin's gone! Aw!

Meet *do*-Pentatonic

"Cookie" is a *do*-pentatonic song because it has five different pitches and it ends on *do*. What are the other pitches?

Sing *do*-Pentatonic

Sing the calls with pitch syllables as your partner sings the responses with pitch syllables. **Play** this rhythm during the responses on the first and second lines.

Calypso music originally came from Trinidad. Some instruments used in calypso music are steel drums, guitar, and maracas.

Singing for Fun!

Some songs are for having fun! *"Piñon, pirulín"* accompanies a game played in Central America. **Sing** the song and **listen** for clues about how to play the game.

CD 6–33
MIDI 10

Piñon, pirulín

English Words by Ellen Traeger

Folk Song from Central America

1. Pi - ñon, pi - ñon, pi - ñon,
1. My friend, my friend, my friend,

pi - ru - lín, pi - ru - lín pi - ru - le - ro.
pi - ru - lín, pi - ru - lín pi - ru - le - ro,

Pi - ñon, pi - ñon, pi - ñon,
He plays u - pon the flute,

pi - ru - lín, pi - ru - lín, pi - ru - lón.
pi - ru - lín, pi - ru - lín, pi - ru - lón.

2. Miguel, Miguel, Miguel,
   que la vuelta está a la derecha.
   Miguel, Miguel, Miguel,
   que la vuelta está al revés.

2. Miguel, Miguel, Miguel,
   To the right, to the right, pick a partner.
   Miguel, Miguel, Miguel,
   To the left, to the left, pick a friend.

Get with the Pitches

"Piñon, pirulín" has five different pitches and ends on *do*. What scale is this? (Hint: *do* is part of the name!) **Sing** the pitch syllables from the song and show hand signs.

do   re   mi   so   la

Sing this pentatonic pattern in between the verses of "Piñon, pirulín."

so   la   so   mi   do   re   so   do

Get with the Rhythm

Play these ostinatos to accompany *"Piñon, pirulín."* Tap and say the rhythm, then **play** the rhythm on the instrument shown.

Folk Style

Look at the folk instruments shown below. **Listen** for them in *El tilingo lingo*.

CD 6–40

El tilingo lingo

Traditional Mexican

El tilingo lingo is a song about dancing. The words describe the sound of the instruments and the beauty of the dances.

The Mexican folk harp has more than 30 strings. ▼

The *requinto* [reh-KEEN-toh] is a smaller guitar with only four strings. ▼

Show What You Know!

Find *do* in each of these phrases.

Sing each phrase with pitch syllables and show hand signs.

The *jarana* [ha-RAH-nah] is a guitar with eight strings. ▼

Sounds of Dixieland

New Orleans was the early home of Dixieland jazz. Woodwind and brass instruments are an important part of this style of music. **Listen** to the song. What instruments do you hear?

CD 6–41
MIDI 11

When the Saints Go Marching In

African American Spiritual

1. Oh, when the saints _____ go march-ing in, _____

Oh, when the saints go march - ing in, _____

Oh, Lord I want to be in that num - ber _____

When the saints go march - ing in.

2. Oh, when the stars
   refuse to shine, . . .

3. Oh, when I hear
   that trumpet sound, . . .

A Jazz Great

Listen to Louis Armstrong's performance of *When the Saints Go Marching In.* What instruments do you hear?

CD 6–43

When the Saints Go Marching In

Traditional Dixieland Tune

Louis Armstrong's audiences loved this song. They often asked him to perform it.

M·U·S·I·C M·A·K·E·R·S
Louis Armstrong

Louis Armstrong (1900–1971) was born in New Orleans. His nickname was "Satchmo." He was a trumpet player, singer, and band leader. Louis Armstrong is one of the most important people in the history of jazz.

Hear a Little Salsa

"Cheki, morena" is a singing game from Puerto Rico. **Listen** to the song. Which instruments can you **identify**? Now **sing** the song and play the game.

CD 7–1
MIDI 12

Cheki, morena

(Shake It!)

English Words by Alice D. Firgau   *Singing Game from Puerto Rico*

Che - ki   mo - re - na,   che - ki,
Shake it,   come on   now,   shake   it!

Che - ki   mo - re - na,   ¡Jue!
Shake it,   come on,   say   hey!

¿Que a dón - de es - ta e - se   rit - mo   ca - ram - ba
I   want   to   hear   the   rhyth - m,   ca - ram - ba,

del   me - re - cum - be?
of   the me - re - cum - be.

Salsa!

Listen to *Vaya Puente*. Name the instruments that you hear. This style of music is called *salsa*.

CD 7–5
Vaya Puente

by Tito Puente

The solo on this recording is played on a trombone.

Un pa - si - to a - lan - te
Take a little step for - ward,

Yo - tro pa - ra tras
Take a little step back,

Y dan - do la vuel - ta dan - do la vuel - ta
and turn - ing a - round and turn - ing a - round you

¿Quién se que - da - ra? ¡Jue!
know you've got the knack. Hey!

A New Kind of Ostinato

Sing this folk song and learn to play the game. To begin, form a circle with one person in the middle.

 CD 7–6 ## The Farmer's Dairy Key

Folk Song from the United States

1. I lost the far - mer's dai - ry key,

I'm in this la - dy's gar - den.

Do, do, let me out

I'm in this la - dy's gar - den.

2. A brass key and a silver lock, . . .

3. A corn stalk fiddle and shoe string bow, . . .

Video Library Watch *One Voice, Many Voices.* Listen to another song with melodic ostinatos.

Ostinato with a Melody

When an ostinato has a melody, it is called a melodic ostinato. **Sing** this melodic ostinato as the rest of the class sings the song. **Describe** the texture. How many layers are there?

do-

Let me out!

Review, Assess,

What Do You Know?

Read the pitches in the song "Cookie" on page 172.

a. Find all the pitches called *so*.

b. Find all the pitches called *la*.

c. Find all the pitches called *mi*.

d. Find all the pitches called *re*.

e. Find all the notes called *do*.

What Do You Hear? 5

CD 7–8

You will hear four musical examples. Decide which instrument is playing in each example.

1.

2.

3.

4.

Perform, Create

What You Can Do

Perform Rhythms

Say these rhythm patterns, using rhythm syllables.

a.

b.

c.

Create an Accompaniment

Choose one of the rhythms above. Play it with "The Farmer's Dairy Key" on page 182.

- What instrument could you use to play your accompaniment?

- How many times will you need to play the pattern to accompany the song?

Create a Dance

Think of a new way to do the "Dinosaur Dance" on page 168. Move one way for the **A** section and a different way for the **B** section.

Stompin' to the Beat

Jazz is a style of music. Jazz invites musicians to make each song they perform their own.

Listen to the recording of *Ja-Da* played by trumpeter Al Hirt.

186

MAKING MUSIC OUR OWN

CD 7–12

Ja-Da

by Bob Carleton
as performed by Al Hirt and his Orchestra

Al Hirt played with many great musicians including Benny Goodman, Tommy Dorsey, and Jimmy Dorsey. He played at the inauguration of President John F. Kennedy, and for Pope John Paul II.

Silence Can Be Interesting!

The song "Ja-Da" has a melody with many silent places. Ask your ear to find them. Then **create** ways to capture the mood of this song. Fill the silences by improvising with body percussion sounds and movements.

Ja-Da

Words and Music by Bob Carleton

Ja - Da, Ja - Da,

Ja - Da, Ja - Da, Jing, Jing, Jing. ___

Ja - Da, Ja - Da,

Ja - Da, Ja - Da, Jing, Jing, Jing. ___

That's a fun-ny lit-tle bit of mel - o - dy. __

It's so sooth-ing and ap-peal-ing to me, __

It goes Ja - Da, Ja - Da,

Ja - Da, Ja - Da, Jing, Jing, Jing. __

CD 7–15

After You've Gone

by Henry Creamer and Turner Layton
as performed by the Benny Goodman Orchestra

M·U·S·I·C M·A·K·E·R·S

Benny Goodman

Benny Goodman (1909–1986) began playing the clarinet at age 10. By 1938 he became the first musician ever to bring jazz to the world-famous stage of Carnegie Hall. That concert brought new interest and respect to jazz as a musical form. Mr. Goodman was widely known as "The King of Swing."

Sing a Story

Listen to the words of "But the Cat Came Back." What is Freddie Wilson's problem? How does he try to solve it?

CD 7–16

But the Cat Came Back

Words and Music by Josef Marais

1. Fred-die Wil-son had a cat that he did-n't want to keep.

He of-fered him for free and he tried to sell him cheap.

He called up-on the preach-er one Sun-day for ad - vice;

The preach-er said, "Yes, leave him here, it would be so nice!"

Soft, Loud, . . . Hold!

Now **sing** the verses softly and the refrain loudly.

Find the note with the **fermata** and hold it for a long time with your whole body. Then decide how to **move** to the refrain.

A **fermata** ⌢ tells a performer to hold a note for an extra long time.

REFRAIN

f But the cat came back, he would-n't stay a - way,

He was sit - tin' on the porch on the ver - y next day.

The cat came back, he did - n't want to roam,

The ver - y next day it was "Home, Sweet Home."

2. Freddie put him on a ship and they headed for Ceylon.
   The ship was overloaded more than twenty thousand ton.
   Not far away from shore the cargo ship went down,
   There wasn't any doubt about it, everybody drowned. *Refrain*

3. Then he put the cat aboard with a man in a balloon,
   Who would give the cat away to the man in the moon.
   The balloon it didn't rise, it burst in bits instead,
   And ten miles from the spot, they found the man stone dead. *Refrain*

Rhythms in Three

Listen to *"Caballito blanco."* How many beats are in each measure? Which is the strongest beat?

Listen to *"Caballito blanco"* again. Use this pattern to keep the steady beat.

pat   snap   snap

Your Own Three-Beat Pattern

Create other ways to play the three-beat pattern. **Play** your pattern as you sing the song.

Caballito blanco
(Little White Pony)

English Words by Bryan Louiselle   *Folk Song from Mexico*

1. Ca - ba - lli - to   blan - co,
1. Take me, dear white   po - ny,

sá - ca - me   de a - quí. _____
Take me far   a - way, _____

C   G

Llé - va - me a   mi   pueb - lo
Back   to   my   own   vil - lage

dón - de   yo   na - cí. _____
Where I   long   to   stay. _____

2. Tengo, tengo, tengo,
    tu no tienes nada.
    Tengo tres borregas
    en una manada.

2. I have quite a fortune,
    You don't have a penny.
    I've three lambs to care for;
    You do not have any.

3. Una me da leche,
    otra me da lana,
    Y otra mantequilla,
    para la semana.

    Repeat verse 1

3. One gives milk each morning,
    One provides her wool,
    One whose gift of butter
    Keeps the larder full.

    Repeat verse 1

Moving in Twos and Threes

Lullabies are soft, gentle songs that people sing to help babies sleep. "Boysie" is a lullaby from Trinidad, an island in the Caribbean Sea.

Pretend you are rocking a baby to sleep. As you **listen** to the song, sway left and right on the strong beats. How many beats do you feel before you sway again?

Left

Right

Lullaby in Three

As you sing "Boysie," tap your feet lightly.
Feel the pattern of three beats in each measure.

CD 7–25

Boysie

Lullaby from Trinidad

Rock,   a rock, a rock, Boy - sie,   Boy - sie   can't sleep;

Rock,   a rock, a rock, Boy - sie,   Boy - sie   can't sleep.

Fine

Look   up - town, look   down - town, find   Boy - sie   there;

Look   up - hill, look   down - hill, find   Boy - sie   there.

D.C. al Fine

Lullaby in Two

"Sleep, Baby, Sleep" is another lullaby. It is in **meter** in two. What is the meter of "Boysie?"

Move with streamers to show the meter of "Sleep, Baby, Sleep."

Meter is the way the beats of music are grouped together. They are often in sets of two or sets of three.

Time to Sleep

As you **sing** "Sleep, Baby, Sleep," pretend to rock a baby.

CD 7–27

Sleep, Baby, Sleep

Lullaby
Adapted by Cheryl Warren-Mattox

1. Sleep, sleep, ba - by sleep, _____
2. Sleep, sleep, ba - by sleep, _____

Go through dream - land's path.
Do just as I say.

But I warn you, yes ___ I do,
Go to sleep, sleep, ba - by sleep,

That the tor - toise is ver - y near.
And the tor - toise will go a - way.

Yes the tor - toise is ver - y near. _____
Yes the tor - toise will go a - way. _____

3. Sleep, sleep, baby sleep,
Dream sweet dreams.
You are safe, Mommy is here,
I will always be very near.
Yes I'll always be very near.

One, Two, Three, Read!

"Un, deux, trois" is a traditional clapping game from France. **Sing** the song and play the game that goes with it!

CD 7–31

Un, deux, trois
(One, Two, Three)
Singing Game from France

Un,   deux,   trois   main   droite.
One,   two,   three   right   hand.

Un,   deux,   trois   main   gauche.
One,   two,   three   left   hand.

Un,   deux,   trois   main   droite,   main   gauche   et
One,   two,   three   right   hand,   left   hand   and

1.
un,   deux,   trois   les   deux.
one,   two,   three   both   hands.

2.
un,   deux,   trois   les   deux.
one,   two,   three   both   hands.

Read the Song

"Un, deux, trois" has three rhythms that you know: ♩ , ♫ , and 𝄽 .

Read the song with rhythm syllables.

Here are two rhythm patterns to accompany *"Un, deux, trois."* **Play** one of the patterns as the class sings the song.

Sing It Again

When you **sing** "Shoo, Fly," there is a special thing you need to do. When you get to the end of the song, you will see the words **D.C. al Fine.** What do you do?

D.C. al Fine is an Italian phrase that tells you to go back to the beginning of the song and sing until the word Fine [FEE-neh].

CD 7–38

Shoo, Fly

Folk Song from the United States

do

Shoo, fly, don't both - er me, Shoo, fly, don't both - er me,

Fine

Shoo, fly, don't both - er me, For I be-long to some-bod - y.

I feel, I feel, I feel, I feel like a morn-ing star,

D.C. al Fine

I feel, I feel, I feel, I feel, I feel like a morn-ing star. So,

A New Form

After you **sing** "Shoo, Fly," decide which picture shows the form of the song.

by Dorothy Aldis

Flies walk on ceilings
And straight up the walls
Not even the littlest
Fly ever falls.

And I am quite certain
If *I* were a fly
I'd leave my home to go
Walk on the sky.

Have you ever had shoo fly pie? Traditionally, Amish children are assigned "guard duty" to shoo away flies as the pie cools on the window sill.

A Mountain of a FORM

This song has one section, **A**. **Sing** the song to discover its message.

CD 7–40

Trouble Is a Mountain

Words and Music by Arthur Cunningham

Trou-ble is a moun-tain, high-er than the sky.

You can climb it, if you try. ___

If you try, ___ if you try, ___

If you try, ___ if you try, ___

You can climb it if you try! ___

Beyond ABA Form

Create new music to play after singing the song and call it **B**. What would you call the form of the music now?

Create more new music and call it **C**. Then **perform** the music in this order.

- Sing the song.
- Play the **B** music.
- Sing the song again.
- Play the **C** music.
- Sing the song.

How would you **describe** the new form?

MUSIC MAKERS

Arthur Cunningham

Arthur Cunningham (1928–1997) was a composer and teacher. His students loved him very much. He believed you can do anything if you try hard enough. Cunningham wrote the song "Trouble Is a Mountain" for the students at Upper Nyack Elementary School in New York.

Pitches in the House

Sing "Great Big House." How many different pitches are in the song?

 CD 7–42

Great Big House

Play-Party Song from Louisiana

Great big house in New Or-leans, For-ty sto-ries high, ___

Eve-ry room that I've been in, Filled with pump-kin pie.

2.   Went down to the old mill stream
   To fetch a pail of water;
   Put one arm around my wife,
   The other 'round my daughter.

3.   Fare thee well, my darling girl,
   Fare thee well, my daughter;
   Fare thee well, my darling girl,
   With golden slippers on her.

Pentatonic House

The five different pitches in "Great Big House" are shown on the staff below. On what pitch does the song end? This pitch is called the home tone.

do   re   mi   so   la

Sing It Again!

Now **sing** "Great Big House" with pitch syllables and hand signs.

Mystery Melodies

Solve this mystery. **Sing** these melodies with pitch syllables. Then see if you can name each song.

1.

so so la la so so mi so so mi mi re   so so la la so so mi so mi re mi do

2.

mi re do re mi so re do re mi   mi re do re mi so re mi re   do

Create your own *do*-pentatonic melody. Choose one of the rhythms below. Make sure your melody ends on *do*, the home tone.

Write your melody on a staff and teach it to a partner.

MELODIC UPS AND DOWNS

Sing "See-Saw Sacradown." What happens to the melody on the words *up* and *down*?

CD 7–49

See-Saw Sacradown

Traditional Rhyme

Music by Paul Kapp

See - Saw Sacradown,

Which is the way to Lon - don town?

One foot up, the oth - er foot down,

That is the way to Lon - don town.

Add an Ostinato

Play this melodic ostinato with "See-Saw Sacradown."

Xylophone

Play a Pentatonic Melody

Play "See-Saw Sacradown." Here are the pitches you need.

Tune In

"See-Saw Sacradown" is a Mother Goose rhyme. Children have used this rhyme to keep time on a see-saw.

Melody Train

Listen to "Chicka Hanka," an African American work song. Then **sing** the song.

Play an Ostinato

Play this melodic ostinato as the class sings the song.

Xylophone

When two trains use the same track, sometimes one has to take the "side track" and wait for the other to pass.

CD 8–1

Chicka Hanka

African American Work Song

Call
Em

do

Cap - tain, go side - track your train! _

Response
Em

Fine

Chick - a hank - a, chick - a hank - a, chick - a hank - a, chick - a

Call
Am   Em

Cap - tain, go side - track your train! _
hank - a.

Response
Em

Chick - a hank - a, chick - a hank - a, chick - a hank - a, chick - a

Call
Em

D.C. al Fine

Num - ber three in line a - com - in' in on time.
hank-a.

Plugged-in Sound

Some instruments depend on electricity for sound. Can you name any?

The theremin was one of the first electronic instruments. It was created about 1919 by a Russian inventor, Leon Theremin. It can make spooky music, like the kind you hear in scary movies.

Listen to Lydia Kavina playing *Free Music #1*.

CD 8–3

Free Music #1

by Percy Grainger

Kavina controls the sound of the theremin by moving her hands over two antennae.

MUSIC MAKERS

Lydia Kavina

Lydia Kavina (born 1967) came from Russia. She began studying with Leon Theremin when she was nine years old and started giving concerts when she was 14. Now she is one of the leading theremin players in the world.

▲ Lydia Kavina, age 9, with Leon Theremin.

Electronic Keyboard Experiment with different sounds on a synthesizer. Invent interesting ways to combine sounds.

LOTS AND LOTS OF LAYERS

Play this accompaniment as the class sings "Rosie, Darling Rosie." Notice how your hands move together to play this ostinato.

Can I play the conga?

Bass Xylophone

Rhythm Texture

Play the rhythm of the words on these instruments to make a thicker texture.

Ro - sie, dar-ling Ro - sie

Ha - ha, Ro - sie

ROSIE, DARLING ROSIE

African American Game Song

Solo
C   G   *Chorus* C   G

1. Ro - sie, dar - ling Ro - sie,   Ha - ha,   Ro - sie;
2. Ro - sie, dar - ling Ro - sie,   Ha - ha,   Ro - sie;

Solo
C   Am   *Chorus* C   G

Ro - sie, dar - ling Ro - sie,   Ha - ha,   Ro - sie;
Ro - sie, dar - ling Ro - sie,   Ha - ha,   Ro - sie;

Solo
C   *Chorus* C   G

Way down yon - der in Bal - ti - more, __ Ha - ha,   Ro - sie;
Come a - long __ and fol - low me, __ Ha - ha,   Ro - sie;

Solo
C   G   *Chorus* C   G

Need no car - pet on my floor, __ Ha - ha,   Ro - sie.
Let's go down to Gal - i - lee, __ Ha - ha,   Ro - sie.

Create a

There is an African story called *The Animals Find Water*. In it, a lion helps the jungle animals dig a well. First he dances while the drummer plays. When he gets tired, he encourages the other animals to take his place. As the animals take turns dancing, the hole gets deeper and deeper until finally, water comes gushing forth!

Create a play of the story with your class.

Lion's Tale

Sing the Lion's Song

Here is a song you can **sing** as part of the play.

CD 8–7
MIDI 13

Kou ri lengay
(The Strength of the Lion)

Words by Ague Commari

Game Song from Tanzania

Kou ri len-gay! Ka-len-gan-a chum, chum, pah!

Kou ri len-gay! Ka-len-gan-a chum, chum, pah!

Kou ri len-gay! Ka-len-gan-a chum, chum, pah!

Kou ri len-gay! Ka-len-gan-a chum, chum, pah!

Four times

O the strength of the li-on is in his tail.

Jungle Rhythms

Here are two ostinatos you can **play** to accompany *"Kou ri lengay."*

Mon-key, mon-key, danc - ing.

Great gray el - e - phant.

Now **create** an ostinato of your own to accompany the song.

Jungle Textures

To add another layer to the accompaniment, **play** this ostinato on a xylophone.

Now **improvise** another layer, using only the pitches shown in white below.

To **improvise** means to make up music as it is being performed.

Review, Assess,

What Do You Know?

1. Match the following words with the correct definitions.

   a. *fermata*

   b. *do* pentatonic

   c. *D.C. al Fine*

   • Go back to the beginning of the song and sing until the word *Fine*.

   • Hold a note for an extra long time.

   • A song that ends on *do* and has five different pitches

2. Read each rhythm pattern below. Find the number of beats in each pattern.

   a. ♫ ♫ = **?**   **c.** ♫ ♩ ♩ = **?**

   b. ♩ 𝄽 ♫ ♩ = **?**   **d.** ♩ ♬ ♩ = **?**

What Do You Hear? 6

 CD 8–10

Listen to the three musical examples. Which set of symbols shows the form of the music?

1. Ⓐ Ⓑ Ⓐ   Ⓐ Ⓑ
2. Ⓐ Ⓑ Ⓐ   Ⓐ Ⓑ
3. Ⓐ Ⓑ Ⓐ   Ⓐ Ⓑ

Perform, Create

What You Can Do

Sing a Melody

Find the song "Great Big House" on page 204. Sing one verse of the song, using pitch syllables and hand signs.

Play an Ostinato

Now play the following ostinato as an accompaniment for "Great Big House."

Create a New Section

Improvise a four-measure **B** section for "Great Big House." Use the pitches shown below. What rhythms will you use?

PATHS TO
Making
Music

Sights and Sounds of American Music

In these pictures, musicians are playing many different kinds of music. Talk about what you see. As you **listen**, match the music you hear with the pictures.

CD 8–13

American Music Styles Sound Montage

Music USA

In the United States, people enjoy music from all over the world. What kinds of music do you like?

Many Kinds of Music

Sing this song. Listen for musical sounds from around the world.

CD 8–14 MIDI 14

Ev'ry Kind of Music

Words and Music by David Eddleman

Ev-'ry kind of mu - sic,   Got-ta have mu - sic,

Give me lots of mu - sic   to   sing and dance and   play. ____

Feel the beat a-mov - in',   Sing-in' a song to make my day,

Makes me swing   and   sway   sing-in' on the way. _____

America Loves Music

People show how they like music in different ways. How does the person in this poem express her feelings about music?

Way Down in the Music

by Eloise Greenfield

I get way down in the music
Down inside the music
I let it wake me
       Take me
Spin me around and make me
Uh—get down

I get way down in the music
Down inside the music
I let it wake me
       Take me
Spin me around and shake me
I get down, down
I get down

FRIENDS Around the Country

Friends share their ideas and feelings. **Sing** this song about friends cooperating to try new things.

 CD 8–16

Glad to Have a Friend Like You

Words and Music by Carol Hall

VERSE

1. Jill told Bill that it was lots of fun to cook.

Bill told Jill that she could bait a real fish-hook.

So they made oo - ey goo - ey choc - olate
And they sat by the riv - er and they

cake stick - y lick - y sug - ar
fished in the wa - ter and they

top and they gob - bled it and gig - gled.
talked as the squirm - y worm - ies wig - gled.

REFRAIN

Sing - in', Glad to have a friend like you,

fair, and fun, and skip - pin' free.

Glad to have a friend like you, and

glad to just be me.

2. Peg told Greg she liked to make things out of chairs.
   Greg told Peg sometimes he still hugged teddy bears.
     So they sneaked in the living room and piled all the pillows up and
     Made it a rocket ship to fly in.
     And the bears were their girls and boys and they were the astronauts
     Who lived on the moon with one pet lion.
   Refrain

Free to Be . . .

Talk about the kinds of things you like to do with your friends. What makes your friends special to you?

Create a Verse

Think of two names that rhyme. Use them to **create** a new verse that fits the rhythm of "Glad to Have a Friend Like You."

Tune In

Free to Be . . . You and Me is an Emmy Award-winning television show. "Glad to Have a Friend Like You" is a song from this show.

Together and Strong

There are many songs about friendship. **Listen** to *Stick Together*. How does this song express the ways friends can help one another?

 CD 8–18
Stick Together

by John McCutcheon and Si Kahn

When John McCutcheon was a young boy he loved music and baseball. As an adult he has been successful in both music and baseball.

 CD-ROM Use music notation software to create a rhythm accompaniment for "Glad to Have a Friend Like You."

Games Americans Play

Folk songs and games are passed down by families and friends. One person teaches another how to sing the song or play the game. Then that person teaches someone else. "Bob-a-Needle" is an African American singing game played in a circle.

CD 8–19

Bob-a-Needle

African American Ring Game

Bob - a - need - le, bob - a - need - le   is   a - run - ning.

Bob - a - need - le, bob - a - need - le   is   a   run - ning,

Bet - ter hide, bob - a - need - le, bob - a - need - le   is   a   run - ning,

Bet - ter hus - tle, bob - a - need - le, bob - a - need - le   is   a   run - ning,

I'll catch bob - a - need - le, bob - a - need - le's not   a   run - ning.

Play the Bob-a-Needle Game

Play the game as you **sing** the song. Each time you repeat the game, sing and **move** at a faster tempo.

Singing on the Trail

Years ago, it took a very long time for people to travel from one place to another as they moved to settle in a new land. Sometimes they sang songs like this one to help pass the time.

CD 8–21 **My Foot's in My Stirrup**

Folk Song from Tennessee

1. My foot's in my stir - rup,

my reins in my hand,

I'm goin' a - way to leave you

Arts Connection

◀ *Untitled* by N.C. Wyeth (1882–1945)

Here is a scene from a day in the life of a cowboy.

for some far dis - tant land.

2. I'm going to Georgia,
   I'm going to Rome,
   I'm going to Georgia
   to make it my home.

3. Go build me a cabin
   on the mountain so high
   Where the wild birds and turtle dove
   can hear my sad cry.

Play Along the Trail

Play these ostinatos as the class sings "My Foot's in My Stirrup." Be sure to keep a steady beat as you play the patterns.

What kinds of sounds would travelers hear on trails in the West? **Create** your own trail sounds.

Cowboy Music

Cowboys also traveled the trail as they moved cattle from one part of the country to another. **Listen** to *The Big Country*. Find the parts in the listening map where the cowboys are moving the cattle as fast as they can. Then, find the parts where they are taking a break.

CD 8–23

The Big Country

by Jerome Moross
The Big Country was the theme music for a cowboy movie made in 1958.

The Big Country
Listening Map

Scene 1

Scene 2

Scene 3

Scene 4

Two American Styles

This singing game dates back to the late 1800s. **Sing** the song, then learn the game.

CD 8–24

A-Tisket, A-Tasket

Folk Song from the United States

A - tis - ket, a - tas - ket, a green and yel - low bas - ket,

I wrote a let - ter to my love and on the way I lost it,

I lost it, I lost it, and on the way I lost it,

a lit - tle dog - gie picked it up and put it in his pock - et.

Jazzin' Up a Song

Listen to this version of *A-Tisket, A-Tasket*.

Compare the singing styles in both recordings.

CD 8–26

A-Tisket, A-Tasket

Folk Song from the United States as adapted and sung by Ella Fitzgerald

Fitzgerald first sang her jazz version of *A-Tisket, A-Tasket* when she was only 18 years old.

M·U·S·I·C M·A·K·E·R·S

Ella Fitzgerald

Ella Fitzgerald (1918–1996) started making music when she was a child. People loved hearing her sing. She became very famous and sang jazz all over the world. She once starred in a television commercial where she sang a note that broke a crystal glass.

Shining from the Inside

When something makes you very happy, you "shine"! Why are the people in these photos "shining"? As you **sing** this song, think about something that makes you "shine."

CD 8–27

We're All Gonna Shine Tonight

Camp Song from the United States

We're all gon-na shine to-night, we're all gon-na shine.

We're all gon-na shine to-night, all down the line.

We're all dressed up to-night; we're feel - ing fine. When the

sun goes down and the moon comes up, We're all gon-na shine.

Shining Sounds

Choose instruments that have a "shining" sound.
Here are some rhythm patterns to **play**.

Let Your Light Shine

Listen to this African American spiritual.
How do you let your light shine?

CD 8–29
This Little Light of Mine

Traditional African American

This song celebrates everyone's special qualities.

Express Yourself

What feelings are expressed in this spiritual? **Sing** "I Got Shoes." Use dynamics, such as *crescendos*, to express the feelings of the song.

CD 8–30
MIDI 15

I Got Shoes

African American Spiritual

Swing Style
Solo

1. I got shoes, _ you got shoes, _

All God's chil - dren got shoes;

Chorus

When I get to heav-en, gon-na put on my shoes; _ I'm gon-na

walk all o - ver God's heav - en, _____

Heav - en, _____ Heav - en; _____

Ev - 'ry - bod - y talk - in' 'bout heav - en ain't go - in' there,

Heav - en, _____ Heav - en, _____ Gon - na

walk all o - ver God's heav - en. _____

2. I got a song, you got a song,
   All God's children got a song;
   When I get to heaven,
     gonna sing my song;
   I'm gonna sing
     all over God's heaven, . . .
   Gonna sing all over God's heaven.

3. I got wings, you got wings,
   All God's children got wings;
   When I get to heaven,
     gonna put on my wings;
   I'm gonna fly
     all over God's heaven, . . .
   Gonna fly all over God's heaven.

TEXAS
Play-Party

Long before radio, television, and movies, people got together and danced for entertainment. These dances were called play-parties.

Sing this play-party from Texas.

CD 8–32
MIDI 16

Shake Them 'Simmons Down

Play-Party Song from Texas

1. Cir - cle right, do - oh, do - oh,
2. Cir - cle left, do - oh, do - oh,

Cir - cle right, do - oh, do - oh,
Cir - cle left, do - oh, do - oh,

Cir - cle right, do - oh, do - oh,
Cir - cle left, do - oh, do - oh,

Shake them 'sim - mons down.
Shake them 'sim - mons down.

3. Boys to the center, do-oh, do-oh, . . .

4. Girls to the center, do-oh, do-oh, . . .

5. Promenade all, do-oh, do-oh, . . .

6. Swing your corner, do-oh, do-oh, . . .

Shake and Sing

The percussion instruments below are played by shaking them. Choose an instrument. Take turns playing it while the class sings the song. You can **play** a steady beat or the rhythm of words.

Fruit Shakers

Maracas

You Can Dance

"Shake Them 'Simmons Down" is a play-party dance you can learn.

Music from Puerto Rico

Flowers love to grow in the warm and sunny climate of Puerto Rico. Spanish is the main language spoken in Puerto Rico, an island in the Caribbean Sea. Did you know that it is part of the United States?

Sing *"El florón,"* a game from Puerto Rico.

CD 9–1
MIDI 17

El florón (The Flower)

English Words by Verne Muñoz   *Singing Game from Puerto Rico*

A   C

El flo - rón   pas - ó   por   a - quí,
Pass the flow - er round and   a - round.

C

Yo   no   lo   vi,   Yo   no   lo   vi.
Will   it   be found?   Will   it   be found?

B   F   C

¿Que pa - se,   que pa - se,
Where is   it?   Where is   it?

G₇   C

Que   pa - se   el   flo - rón? _____
Where can   the   flow - er   be? _____

246

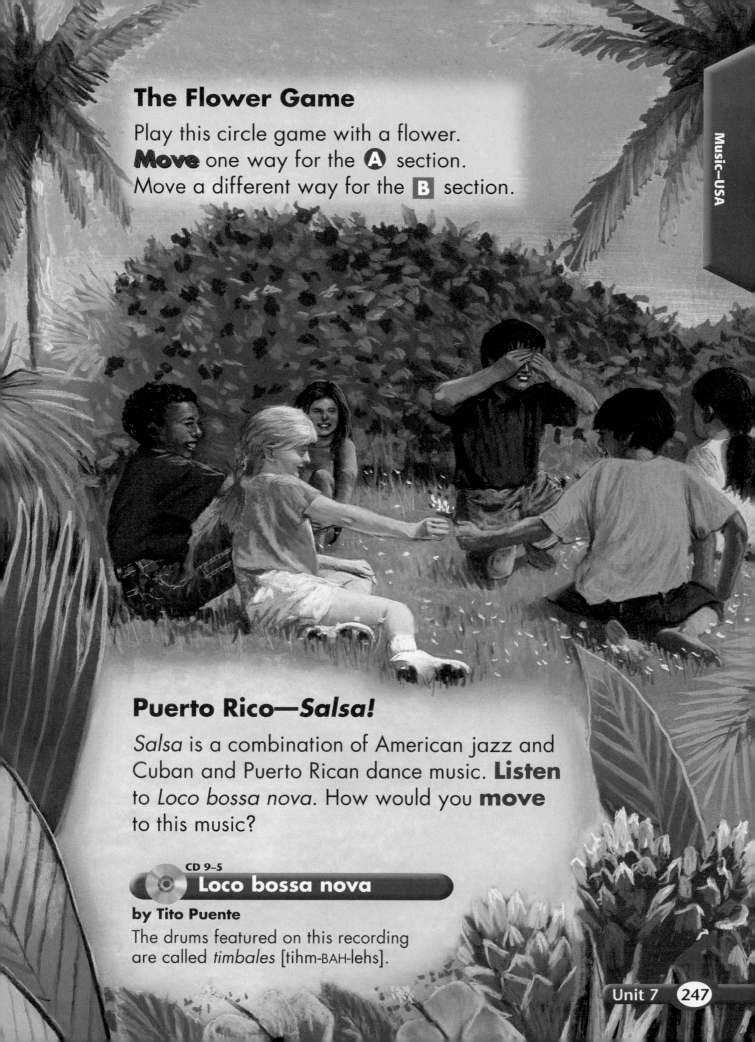

The Flower Game

Play this circle game with a flower.
Move one way for the **A** section.
Move a different way for the **B** section.

Puerto Rico—*Salsa!*

Salsa is a combination of American jazz and Cuban and Puerto Rican dance music. **Listen** to *Loco bossa nova.* How would you **move** to this music?

CD 9–5
Loco bossa nova

by Tito Puente
The drums featured on this recording are called *timbales* [tihm-BAH-lehs].

Music of the First Americans

Each Native American tribe in the United States has its own music.

Sing this song of the Wechihit-Yokuts of California. They believe that the eagle is the most powerful of all birds.

CD 9–6

Song of the Eagle

Native American Song of the Wechihit

Heh - weh - yeh kah - ah - wah

Heh - weh - yeh kah - wah

ah wah - kah-ah chah_ choh - cheh leh mah nohn.

Powwow Dance

Move to the steady beat as you sing "Duck Dance." This Choctaw and Seminole song is performed at powwows.

CD 9-9

Duck Dance

Native American Dance Song of the Seminole and Choctaw

We   he   ya   we   he   ya   he   ya   yo-ah   he   na   he   ya

we   he   ya   he   ya   yo-a   ha   na   he   ya   we   he   ya   he   na

The Snake Dance is a Florida Seminole stomp dance. ▶

Ragtime RHYTHMS

Ragtime music was very popular over a hundred years ago, in the 1890s. People loved to dance to its unique rhythms. **Listen** to the song "Ragtime Cowboy Joe." **Move** with the feeling of the music as you **sing** the song.

 CD 9–12

Ragtime Cowboy Joe

Words by Grant Clarke　　　　　　*Music by Lewis F. Muir and Maurice Abrahams*

Swing Style

Oh, how he sings rag-gy mu-sic to his cat-tle

as he swings back and forth in his sad-dle

on a horse that is syn-co-pa-ted, gai-ted.

What a fun-ny me-ter to the roar of his re-pea-ter.

How they run   when they hear the fel-la's gun

be-cause the wes-tern folks all know

He's a high-fa-lu-tin', roo-tin', too-tin',

son-of-a-gun from Ar-i-zon-a,

He's some cow-boy, talk a-bout your cow-boy,

Rag-time Cow-boy Joe.

Cowboy Ragtime

Imagine cowboys moving in their saddles with this rhythm.

Listen to *Kansas City Stomp*. **Create** a dance to match the rhythm of the song. How will you move when the music stops?

CD 9–14

Kansas City Stomp

by Ferdinand 'Jelly Roll' Morton as performed by Morten Gunnar Larsen

Long before the phonograph and electricity were invented, the piano was the most popular instrument for performing ragtime music.

Dancin' USA

In the 1920s, the Charleston was a popular American dance. **Listen** to the song "Happy Feet." **Describe** what you hear. Then **move** along with the song.

CD 9–15

Happy Feet

Words by Jack Yellen

Music by Milton Ager

Hap-py feet! I've got those hap-py feet.
Wear-y blues can't get in - to my shoes.

Give them a low - down beat
Be - cause my shoes re - fuse

And they __ be - gin danc - ing.
to ev - er grow wear - y.

1.

I've got those ten lit - tle tap-ping toes

And _ when they hear a tune, I can't con - trol

My danc - ing heels to save my soul.

2.

I keep cheer-ful _ on an ear-ful _ of mu - sic sweet, _

'Cause I've got hap - hap - hap-py _ feet.

▼ Cab Calloway and his Orchestra

The Motown Sound

Motown is a **style** of rock music. **Listen** to Martha Reeves and the Vandellas sing the Motown hit *Dancing in the Street*.

Motown groups perform special dance moves as they sing. How would you **move** to this song?

Style is the special sound that is created when music elements, such as rhythm and timbre, are combined.

CD 9–17

Dancing in the Street

by Marvin Gaye, William Stevenson, and Ivy Hunter

Motown is named after its hometown, Detroit. Detroit is known as the Motor City because of the many car factories there.

Latin Roots

Many rock bands mix other music styles into their songs. **Listen** to Santana's version of *Oye como va*. It combines rock and roll and *salsa*.

CD 9–18

Oye como va

by Tito Puente
as performed by Santana

The electric guitar is the featured solo instrument played by Carlos Santana.

M·U·S·I·C M·A·K·E·R·S
Carlos Santana

Carlos Santana (born 1947) started playing guitar professionally when he was 13 years old. He has been the leader of the band Santana since the late 1960s. He won nine Grammy Awards in the year 2000.

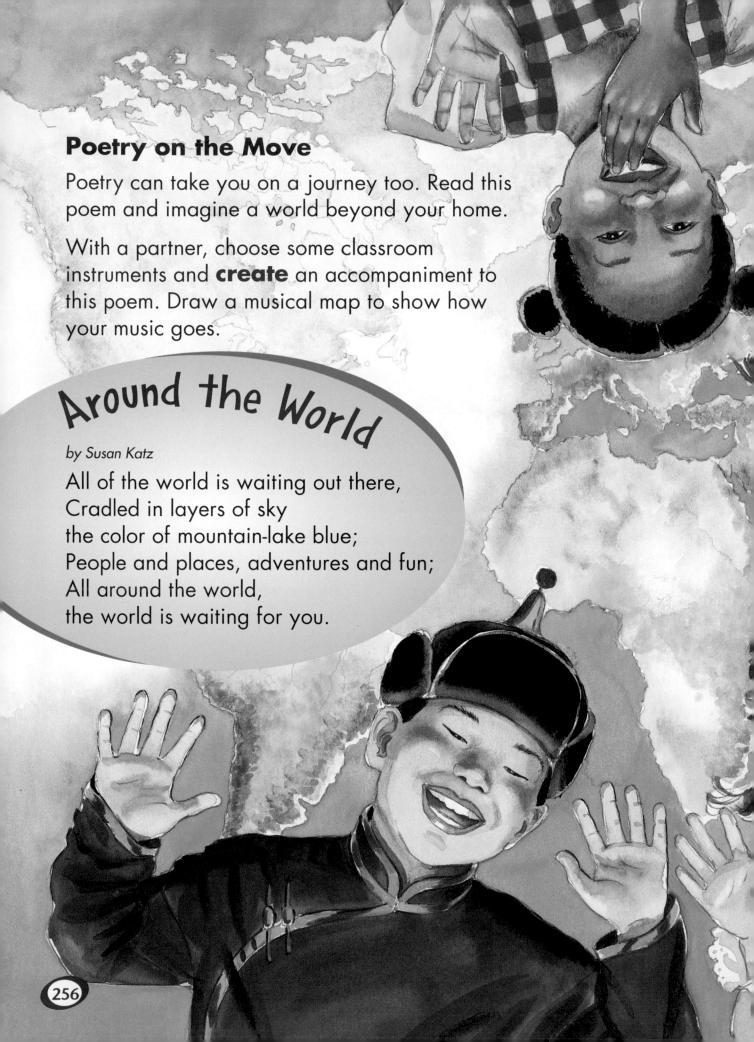

Poetry on the Move

Poetry can take you on a journey too. Read this poem and imagine a world beyond your home.

With a partner, choose some classroom instruments and **create** an accompaniment to this poem. Draw a musical map to show how your music goes.

Around the World

by Susan Katz

All of the world is waiting out there,
Cradled in layers of sky
the color of mountain-lake blue;
People and places, adventures and fun;
All around the world,
the world is waiting for you.

Home and Away

Take a journey around our musical world and discover how music is enjoyed by children everywhere.

A Musical Journey

"All the Way Around the World" is a song about children on a boat journey. **Listen** for the many musical styles in the accompaniment. Then **sing** the song with your class.

CD 9–19

All the Way Around the World

Words and Music by Katherine Dines

VERSE

D

do

1. This boat's gon-na car-ry hap-pi-ness, —
2. This boat's gon-na car-ry har-mo-ny, —

A₇   **D**

hap - pi - ness, —   hap - pi - ness. —
har - mo - ny, —   har - mo - ny. —

D

This boat's gon-na car - ry hap - pi - ness, —
This boat's gon-na car - ry har - mo - ny, —

A₇   **D**

All the way a - round the world.
All the way a - round the world.

REFRAIN

All the way a - round _ the world this

boat's gon - na fly with its sails un - furled,

to ev - 'ry boy and ev - 'ry girl, _____

All the way a - round the world.

3. This boat's gonna carry love and peace, . . .
Refrain

4. This boat's gonna carry hope and strength, . . .
Refrain

Getting There Is

What is your favorite way to travel? In Caracas, Venezuela, people often take trips on trains. As you **listen** to the song "*El tren*," imagine how the train is moving.

CD 9–21

El tren
(The Train)

Folk Song from Venezuela

Call
F

1. "Pa' Ca - ra - cas" di - ce el tren _____
1. "To Ca - ra - cas" says the train _____

C₇ F

cuan - do vie - ne de Los Te - ques,
when it's chug - ging from Los Te - ques,

Response
F

"Pa' Ca - ra - cas" di - ce el tren _____
"To Ca - ra - cas" says the train _____

C₇ F

cuan - do vie - ne de Los Te - ques.
when it's chug - ging from Los Te - ques.

Half the Fun!

Moving Sounds

Create a "soundscape" to show your favorite kind of transportation.

Call

B♭   F

Pa'   Ca - ra - cas,   pa'   Ca - ra - cas,
To   Ca - ra - cas,   to   Ca - ra - cas,

C_7 F

siem - pre   lle - ni - to   de   gen - te
steam   a - puff - ing   from   its   fun - nel.

Response

B♭   F

pa - sa a   ve - ces   por   un   tú - nel
Al - ways   full   of   peo - ple   trav' - ling

C_7 F

y o - tras   ve - ces   por   un   puen - te.
o - ver   brid - ges,   through   a   tun - nel.

2. *Cuando pasa por un túnel*
   siempre va muy lentamente,
  Cuando pasa por un túnel
   siempre va muy lentamente,
  Con cuidado, despacito
   para no "asustar" a la gente,
  Despactio, despacito
   caminando, lentamente.

2. When it's passing through a tunnel
   it goes clanking, slowly clanking;
  When it's passing through a tunnel
   it goes clanking, slowly clanking;
  Never scary, always wary
   as it travels, always puffing.
  It takes care to go more slowly,
   always huffing, always chuffing.

Hello, Friends!

People around the world greet each other in different ways. How do you greet your friends?

Sing "Hello!" and discover new ways to say "hello."

CD 9–25

Hello!

Words and Music by Laszlo Slomovits

REFRAIN

Hel - lo, hel - lo, hel - lo, hi, hi, hi,

Hel - lo, hel - lo, hel - lo, hi!

VERSE

1. In France they say, "Bon-jour," "Bon-jour." *(Echo)*

In Chi-na they say, "Ni hao," "Ni hao." *(Echo)*

In Is-rael they say, "Sha-lom," "Sha-lom." *(Echo)*

Greet with a Beat!

Listen to "Hello!" **Move** around the room to the beat. Each time you hear a new greeting, stop and greet a classmate in a different way.

In South Af - ri - ca _ they say,   "Du - me - la,"   "Du - me - la."

Some-times we shake hands;   we wave   and we grin. _

We pat each oth - er on the back; _ we say, "Hi! How you been?" _

2. In Mexico they say, "Buenos Días," "Buenos Días."
   In Russia they say, "Zdrastvooyti," "Zdrastvooyti."
   In Japan they say, "Konnichi Wa," "Konnichi Wa."
   In India they say, "Namaste," "Namaste." . . .
   Refrain

Greetings from Russia

Listen to Igor Stravinsky talk about how he composed *Greeting Prelude*. Then listen to the music. Do you hear a song you know?

CD 9–27
Interview and Greeting Prelude

by Igor Stravinsky

Stravinsky composed *Greeting Prelude* in 1955 to celebrate the 80th birthday of a good friend.

M·U·S·I·C   M·A·K·E·R·S

Igor Stravinsky

Igor Stravinsky (1882–1971) was born in Russia. Some of his most famous music was for ballet. Later in his life he moved to Hollywood, California. In 1982 his picture was put on a 2¢ postage stamp.

Greetings from Thailand

In the Thai language, if you say *sawatdee* one way, it means "hello." If you say it another way, it means "goodbye."

Follow the direction of the melody in *"Sawatdee tuh jah."* Point to each pitch as you **sing**.

CD 9–28

Sawatdee tuh jah
(The Hello Song)

Folk Song from Thailand
Collected by Mary Shamrock

สวัสดี _____ เธอ จ๋ำ _____ เรา มา พบ กัน
Sah - wat - dee tuh jah __ rao mahn paup gun,
When we meet each oth - er, we say hel - lo.

เธอ เรา กับ _____ ฉัน กัน สวัสดี _____
Tu re chahn _ paup gun sah - wat - dee.
When we meet, __ we say hel - lo.

Follow the Leader

"Che che koolay" is a song from Ghana. It is in call-and-response form. A leader sings first, then everyone answers. Do the leader and the group sing the same melody?

CD 9–32
MIDI 18

Che che koolay

Folk Song from Ghana

Call (C)   Response (R)

Che   che   koo - lay,   Che   che   koo - lay,

(C)   (R)

Che   che   ko - fee   sa,   Che   che   ko - fee   sa,

(C)   (R)

Ko - fee   sa - lan - ga,   Ko - fee   sa - lan - ga.

(C)   (R)

Ka - ka - shee lan - ga,   Ka - ka - shee lan - ga.

(C)   (R)

Whoops!   Ah lye   lye! Whoops!   Ah lye   lye!

Rhythm Chat

With a partner, **create** a call-and-response game. **Clap** one of the "calls" below. Your partner can create a response. Then switch parts.

1.

2.

3.

People in Ghana sometimes use drums to send messages. ▶

GHANA

Element: FORM Skill: MOVING Connection: MATH

Do the Zudio!

People everywhere like to dance to music. It is fun to dance to this song from the United States.

Zudio Moves

Sing the refrain of "Zudio." Think of different ways you can **move** to the beat.

Zudio

Traditional Street Song from the United States

REFRAIN

Here we go zu - di - o, zu - di - o, zu - di - o,

Here we go zu - di - o, all night long. —

Step back, Sal - ly, Sal - ly, Sal - ly,

Step back, Sal - ly, all night long. —

VERSE
Walkin' down the alley, what do I see?
I see a great big man from Tennessee.
Betcha five dollars I can catch that man,
Betcha five dollars I can catch that man.
To the side, to the side, to the side, side, side;
To the side, to the side, to the side, side, side,
Side, side, side.

My mama called the doctor; the doctor said,
       (First time only) "Oo, oh, I got a pain in my head."
       (Second time only) "Oo, oh, I got a pain in my tum."
       (Third time only) "Oo, oh, I got a pain in my side."
To the side, to the side, to the side, side, side;
To the side, to the side, to the side, side, side,
Side, side, side. *Refrain (First and second times only)*

Home and Away

Singing Games HAWAIIAN STYLE

Children from near and far play singing games. *"Kapulu kane"* is a singing game from Hawaii.

Sing the song, and then play the game.

CD 9–37

Kapulu kane
(Puili Game Song)

Singing Game from Hawaii

Ka - pu - lu, pu - lu Ka - ne, Ka - pu - lu, pu - lu Ka - ne,

Ka - pu - lu, pu - lu Ka - ne ku - ka - na - lu - a.

Ka - pu - lu, pu - lu Ka - ne, Ka - pu - lu, pu - lu Ka - ne,

Ka - pu - lu, pu - lu Ka - ne ku - ka - na - lu - a.

Sticks Together

Children in Hawaii use *puili* [poo‿EE-lee] sticks to make music and play games.

▲ *Puili* sticks are made of bamboo. The split ends make a special sound when they are tapped.

Play this *puili* stick game as you **sing** *"Kapulu kane."* Be sure to **tap** on each beat.

Tune In

Hawaii is the newest state in the United States. It is made up of 132 islands.

CIRCLE

Children all over the world play circle games. **Sing** this circle game song from Brazil. Trace the melody as you sing.

Move to show where the phrases begin and end.

CD 10–1

CIRANDA
(A Ring of Roses)

Singing Game from Brazil

Ci - ran - da ci - ran - di - nha,
A ring a ring of ro - ses,

Va - mos to - dos ci - ran - dar.
Let's all dance a - round to - day.

Va - mos dar a me - ia vol - ta,
Let's ___ dance 'round in a cir - cle,

vol - ta e me - ia va - mos dar.
then go back the oth - er way.

Do the Dance!

Form a circle to do the dance.
First skip around to the right.
Then skip around to the left.

‹Arts Connection

Sally Walker by Brenda
Joysmith (born 1953)
shows a popular African
American circle game. ▼

Let's Play the Drum!

"*El tambor*" means "the drum" in Spanish. **Listen** to "*El tambor*." What two rhythms are used in this song?

CD 10–7

El tambor
(The Drum)

Folk Song from Mexico

Un tam - bor, me com - pró
Lit - tle drum, lit - tle drum

el do - min - go mi pa - pá,
my pa - pa bought me to - day,

Y a ju - gar me lle - vó
Lit - tle drum, lit - tle drum

por la tar - de mi ma - má.
my ma - ma taught me to play.

Speaking Rhythms

Look at this ostinato. It also uses quarter notes and eighth notes. **Perform** the ostinato using rhythm syllables.

Choose a partner. Now **clap** the ostinato eight times while your partner sings "El tambor." Then trade parts and **perform** the song again.

Chinese Timbres

▲ zheng   ▲ erhu   ▲ sheng

Listen to this recording of instruments from China. Match the pictures of the instruments with the sounds you hear.

 CD 10–11
Chinese Instruments Montage

 Video Library Watch *From Mao to Mozart: Isaac Stern in China.* See a Chinese student have a lesson on playing the *erhu.*

276

A Game from China

Sing *"Diou shou juan'er."*
Which instruments sound familiar?

CD 10–12

Diou shou juan'er
(Hide the Scarf)

English Words by David Eddleman   *Singing Game from China*

丢 ___ 手 ___ 絹   丢 ___ 手 ___ 絹
Diou __ shou __ juan'er,   *diou __ shou __ juan'er,*
Run the scarf a-round,   Where can it be found?

輕 輕 地 放 在 小 朋 友 的 後 ___ 面
qing qing di fang xai xioa peng you di hou __ bian,
Drop it be-hind some-one who's in the cir - cle;

大 家 不 要 告 訴 他
Da jia bu yao gao su ta,
When it's found you start the chase,

快 點 快 點 抓 住 他
Kai dain'er, kai dain'er, zhua zhu ta.
Catch her and you'll take her place.
(him)   (his)

Dancing Across the Ages

A long time ago, in France, the *pavane* and the *gaillarde* were popular dances. Imagine a big castle ballroom where royal subjects are dancing at an elegant party.

Arts Connection

▲ *Court Ball at the Palais du Louvre* (1582) Flemish School

Ancient Dance Music

Listen to *Pavane et Gaillarde* and follow the listening map.

Identify where the meter changes in the music.

CD 10-16

Pavane et Gaillarde

by Thoinot Arbeau

The *pavane* [pah-VAHN] is a slow dance.
The *gaillarde* [gī-YAHRD] is a dance with jumps and kicks.

Pavane et Gaillarde Listening Map

Pavane

Gaillarde

Folk Dances

The polka started as a folk dance.
It later became a popular ballroom dance.

Sing *"Mon papa."* This French song is about
a girl who wants to dance the polka.

CD 10–17

Mon papa
(My Papa)

English Words by Edith Bicknell

Folk Song from France

1. Mon pa - pa ne veut pas
1. My pa - pa will say no,

Que je dan - se, que je dan - se,
No more danc - ing, no more danc - ing,

Mon pa - pa ne veut pas
My pa - pa will say no,

Que je dan - se la pol - ka!
No more pol - ka danc - ing now!

2. Mais malgré sa défense,
   Moi je danse, moi je danse,
   Mais malgré sa défense,
   Moi je danse la polka!

2. Oh papa, dear papa,
   Let me go and dance the polka,
   Oh papa, dear papa,
   Let me dance the polka now!

You Can Polka Too!

This is a dance you can do with your classmates.

CD 10–21
Patty Cake Polka

Traditional Square Dance Tune

The *Patty Cake Polka* has been danced in the United States for many years.

PLAY-PARTY

Imagine you are at a party in a big barn with decorations all around. The year is about 1870. Now **sing** and dance this play-party from the old days.

SOMEBODY WAITING

Play-Party Song from the United States

1. As I look in-to your eyes, I be-hold a glad sur-prise,

There is some-bod-y wait-ing for me.

2. There is some-bod-y wait-ing, there is some-bod-y wait-ing,

There is some-bod-y wait-ing for me.

3. Now choose two, leave the others, . . . 4. Swing the one, leave the other, . . .

Play-Party Clapping

Clap this rhythm with the song to help keep the play-party moving.

 Video Library Watch *Folk Dance* to learn about other folk dances from around the world.

A Maori Goodbye...

Maori [MOW-ree] people live in New Zealand. They often use hand movements to tell the stories of their songs.

"*Haere*" is a Maori goodbye song. **Perform** these body percussion rhythms with the song.

stamp clap clap clap stamp clap

pat chest snap pat chest snap

Singing Goodbye

Now **sing** *"Haere"* with body percussion rhythms. What is the meter of the song?

CD 10–27

Haere
(Farewell)

English Words by David Eddleman

Maori Song from New Zealand

Hae - re hae - re ra
Find the place you be - long,

kia ka - ha ki - a to - a e
Fare - well, ___ my friend, may you be well.

ki te whe - nu - a i te ta - ha
You must be brave and you must be strong,

o te to - nga e wha - ka - ria nei. ___
Fol - low the light as you trav - el on. ___

Hae - re hae - re ra.
Fare - well, fare - well, my friend, fare - well.

Sing Your Way Home

After a long trip, it is good to get home.

Sing this song about traveling home. **Describe** the form of the song.

CD 10–31
MIDI 20

I'm Flying Home

Words and Music by David Eddleman

VERSE Eb   Eb/Bb   Bb

1. Fly - ing   from   an   east - ern   cit - y, ____
2. Fly - ing   'cross   a   snow - capped   moun - tain, __

Eb   Eb/Bb   Bb

fly - ing   to   a   west - ern   town,
soar - ing   'cross   a   gras - sy   plain,

Eb   Ab/Eb

I   know   an - y - place   I'm   head - ed,
North - west   down   to   south - ern   cli - mate,

Bb7   Eb   *Fine (after verse 4)*

I'm   fly - ing   home.
I'm   fly - ing   home.

Singing Well

As you **sing** the song, remember these two things. Sit up straight and keep your shoulders relaxed.

Fly - ing, fly - ing, let me roam,

An - y - place I go is home.

3. Flying over thirsty desert,
   flying to New England's shore,
   Great Lakes to Southwest and onward,
   I'm flying home. *Refrain*

4. Flying from an eastern city,
   flying to a western town,
   I know anyplace I'm headed,
   I'm flying home. *Refrain*

Walk with the Animals

Choose a favorite animal and **move** the way that animal does as you **sing** "What Do Animals Need?" See if your classmates can guess which animal you are!

CD 10–34

What Do Animals Need?

Words and Music by the
Banana Slug String Band

REFRAIN

do

Em   D   Em

1. What do an - i - mals need?   A wild home. __
2. What does ev - 'ry - one need?   A healthy home. __

Em   Bm₇

What do an - i - mals need?   Room to roam. __
What does ev - 'ry - one need?

Em   D   Em

What do an - i - mals need?   Clean wa - ter and air. __
What does ev - 'ry - one need?

To verses 1., 2., 3.

Em   Bm₇   Em

What do an - i - mals need?   Love and care.
What does ev - 'ry - one need?

288

Creature Feature

Animals are a very important part of our world. Here are some songs about caring for and enjoying the creatures of the land and sea.

Talk with the Animals

Speak this rhythm. Then **play** it with
"What Do Animals Need?"

Save   the Earth   and   ev'-ry-thing that's in   it.

Sing with the Animals

Sing the melody below. **Play** it on a xylophone.

Let's give   the crea-tures what they need.

MUSIC MAKERS

The Banana Slug String Band

The Banana Slug String Band entertains people with music while teaching them about science and ecology. The Slugs are "Airy" Larry Graff, Doug "Dirt" Greenfield, "Solar" Steve Van Zandt, and "Marine" Mark Nolan. They accompany their songs with guitars, mandolin, bass, harmonica, banjo, and percussion.

FROG

Listen for different frog sounds in the song *"El coquí."* Can you create those sounds yourself?

EL COQUÍ
(The Little Frog)

English Words by José-Luis Orozco

Musical arrangement by José-Luis Orozco
Folk Song from Puerto Rico

El co - quí, el co - quí a mí me en - can - ta.
My co - quí, lit - tle frog, how I love you.

Es bo - ni - to el can - tar del co - quí.
For your songs give me com - fort and peace.

Por las no - ches, al ir a a - cos - tar - me
Ev - ery night I can go to sleep hap - py,

Me a dor - me - ce can - tan - do a - sí.
When I hear lull - a - bies from co - quí.

292

MUSIC

Hopping in Three

As you **listen** to "*El coquí*" again, **move** to show the meter.

Tune In

Some frogs sing by squeezing air from their lungs. They keep their nostrils and mouth shut. This makes their vocal sacs puff out like a balloon.

REFRAIN

Co - quí,   co - quí,   co - quí - quí - quí - quí.

Co - quí,   co - quí,   co - quí - quí - quí - quí.

Element: RHYTHM | **Skill: READING** | **Connection: SCIENCE**

Sounds of Nature

Nature creates wonderful music and art. What are some of your favorite sights and sounds in nature? **Sing** this song about wildlife by the waterside.

CD 10–40

Listen to the Water

Words and Music by Bob Schneider

REFRAIN

Lis - ten to the wa - ter, Lis - ten to the wa - ter

Roll - ing down ___ the riv - er. ___

Lis - ten to the wa - ter, Lis - ten to the wa - ter

Roll - ing down ___ the ri - ver. ___

Natural Rhythms

Read these water wildlife names.
Match each name with its rhythm.

1. snake   a.

2. sandpiper   b.

3. snapping turtle c.

VERSE

1.,2. Well, we saw some birds by the wa - ter - side, __
fish

We saw some birds by the wa - ter - side, __
fish

We saw some birds by the wa - ter - side, __
fish

Oh, oh, __ by the wa - ter - side, _____

D.C. al Fine

Oh, oh, __ by the wa - ter - side. __

3. . . . ducks . . .   4. . . . flowers . . .

Creature Feature

Creature Tale

"*Chawe chidyo chem'chero*" is a song story. There are many song stories from Africa. These stories are good for telling around a fire at night.

The Story of the *Kudu*

Listen to this story about a *kudu* who wants to eat a family's garden.

CD 11–1

Chawe chidyo chem'chero

Traditional story from Zimbabwe

Learn how the *kudu* charms the family with his music and gets to eat all he wants.

A *kudu* is an antelope that lives in eastern and southern Africa. *Kudus* have grayish fur, and the male *kudu* has spiral horns.

The *Kudu's* Song

Sing this song with the story.

CD 11–2

Chawe chidyo chem'chero

Shona Ngano Song from Zimbabwe

Cha - we, chi - dyo chem' che - ro

Cha - we, chi - dyo chem' che - ro

Play Along with the Song!

Now **play** this ostinato with the song.

low high high high low   high

Say and **play** this rhythm pattern with the song and story.

Don't eat   the gar - den   Ku - du.

Perform the Story

Perform the story and take turns being the *kudu*. Who will play the other characters? What other animals could be part of the story?

Sing the *kudu's* song during the story. **Play** a drum or **clap** the rhythm you learned with the song.

Be a Cool Cat!

Now, use body percussion to **perform** this rhythm with *"Der sad to katte."*

Saa sa' den e - ne: "Hør min ven,"
Said one, "Now lis - ten here, my friend,"

krit - te - vit - te - vit - te - vit - te - vit bom bom,
krit - te - vit - te - vit - te - vit - te - vit bom bom,

"sku' vi ik - ke krav - le ned i - gen?"
"I ___ think we should get down a - gain,"

krit - te - vit - te - vit bom bom.
krit - te - vit - te - vit bom bom.

2. *Og da de saa var kommet ned,*
   krittevittevit bom bom.
   saa sa' den anden: "Hør min ven,"
   krittevittevit bom bom.
   "sku' vi ikke kravle op igen?"
   krittevittevittevittevit bom bom,
   og saa kravlede de op igen,
   krittevittevit bom bom.

2. They scrambled down and took a rest,
   krittevittevit bom bom.
   The other said, "No, up is best,"
   krittevittevit bom bom.
   So they climbed up that tree again,
   krittevittevittevittevit bom bom,
   And that's a game that has no end,
   krittevittevit bom bom.

A Batty Melody

This folk song tells four creature tales.
Listen to "Leatherwing Bat."
Then move to act out the stories.

Verse 1
. . . heart's delight

Verse 2
. . . dressed in black

Verse 3
. . . head's been red

Verse 4
. . . as he flew

Bats use sound pulses
to find things and to keep
from crashing into them.

Fly with the Melody

Now, sing the song and trace the direction of the melody. It takes the shape of a bat's flight pattern.

CD 11–9

Leatherwing Bat

Folk Song from the British Isles

1. "Hi," said the lit-tle lea-ther-wing bat, "I'll tell you the rea-son that,

The rea-son that I fly by night is be-cause I lost my heart's de-light."

REFRAIN

How-dy, dow-dy did-dle-o-day, How-dy, dow-dy did-dle-o-day,

How-dy, dow-dy did-dle-o-day, How-dy, dow-dy did-dle-o-day.

2. "Hi," said the blackbird,
   sitting on a chair,
   "Once I courted a lady fair;
   She proved fickle and turned her back,
   And ever since then
   I've dressed in black."
   Refrain

3. "Hi," said the woodpecker,
   sitting in the grass,
   "Once I courted a bonny lass;
   She proved fickle and from me fled,
   And ever since then
   my head's been red."
   Refrain

4. "Hi," said the greenfinch as he flew,
   "I loved one that proved untrue;
   And since she will no more be seen,
   Every spring I change to green."
   Refrain

Creature Feature

Rabbit Rhythms

Sing this song about a mother rabbit gathering food for her young.

 CD 11–11
MIDI 21

Rabbit Footprints

Words and Music by David Eddleman

I spy rab - bit foot-prints in the snow,

She is gath - 'ring sup - per, I know,

To feed her lit - tle ones warm in the nest

Be - fore they set - tle down for a cold eve - ning

rest. _____ (hum) _____

Rhythms to Play

Play these rhythm patterns with the song.

Rabbit Thoughts

Read this poem by a twelve-year-old poet.
Then you can write your own rabbit poem.

Rabbits

by Noah Wager

Rabbits come in many colors
caramel, black, and white.
They match the snow,
they match the clouds,
Their fur is clean and bright.

They jump, they skip, they run,
they hop on all four feet.
They gnaw on greens, carrots,
beans, and that is what they eat.

Crabby Lullaby

Many children in Haiti know about crabs. They are all around the beaches and on their dinner tables! **Sing** this lullaby from Haiti, but don't worry. This crab won't really eat anyone's toes!

CD 11–13

Deau-deau, ti pitit maman
(Sleep, My Little One)

English Words by Edith Bicknell

Lullaby from Haiti as sung by Germaine Sorel

Deau - deau, ti pi - tit ma - man.
Deau - deau, sleep my lit - tle one.

Deau - deau, ti pi - tit ma - man.
Deau - deau, sleep my lit - tle one.

Si ou pa Deau-deau, Crab la ap man - gé - ou. ___
Sleep now or, Deau-deau, Crab will eat your toes. ___

Si ou pa Deau-deau, Crab la ap man-gé - ou. ___
Sleep now or, Deau-deau, Crab will eat your toes. ___

Join the Lullaby

Play the accompaniment below while others sing the song.

Metallophone

Arts Connection

◀ *Untitled* by Audes Saul. Look at this painting by an artist from Haiti. Find the crab. What else do you see?

A MUSICAL MENAGERIE

A menagerie [muh-NA-zher-ree] is a group of different animals. **Sing** this folk song from Kentucky about one person's menagerie.

CD 11–17

I Bought Me a Cat

Folk Song from Kentucky

```
                cat,            cat
1.,2.,3.,4.   I  bought  me  a  hen,  and the  hen  pleased me.
                duck,           duck
                goose,          goose
```

```
              cat
I  fed  my   hen   un - der  yon - der   tree.
              duck
              goose
```

Animal Patterns

Practice these patterns. Decide which pattern sounds best for each animal. **Play** your pattern when the animal speaks in the song.

Cat goes *fid - dle - i - fee!* _____

Hen goes *chim-my-chuck, chim-my-chuck!*

Duck goes *quack, quack!*

Goose goes *his - sy, his - sy!*

Worms at Work!

Worms don't often get much credit. But the fact is, red worms can turn trash into great soil for your garden! **Sing** this song about respect for worms.

CD 11–19
MIDI 22

Lots of Worms

Words and Music by Patty Zeitlin

1. Well, there are lots of worms — way un-der the ground, —

Lots of worms — that I've nev-er found. — I'll bet they're

way down there — a-dig-gin' a-round, —

Way un-der the ground. —

2. I dug the biggest hole I ever did dig,
   The biggest hole. It sure was big!
   And when I got to the bottom, you know what I found
   Way under the ground.

3. I found a worm to go on a fishing pole
   Down in the bottom of that deep, dark hole.
   But I left him alone 'cause he liked his home
   Way under the ground.

4. I found a bumpety bug with big black dots,
   Thirty-three legs and twenty-two spots.
   But I left it alone 'cause it liked its home
   Way under the ground.

5. I found an old sow bug curled up like a ball
   She didn't move from there at all.
   So I left her alone 'cause she liked her home
   Way under the ground.
   Repeat verse 1

Earthworm Construction Inc. We aerate soil.

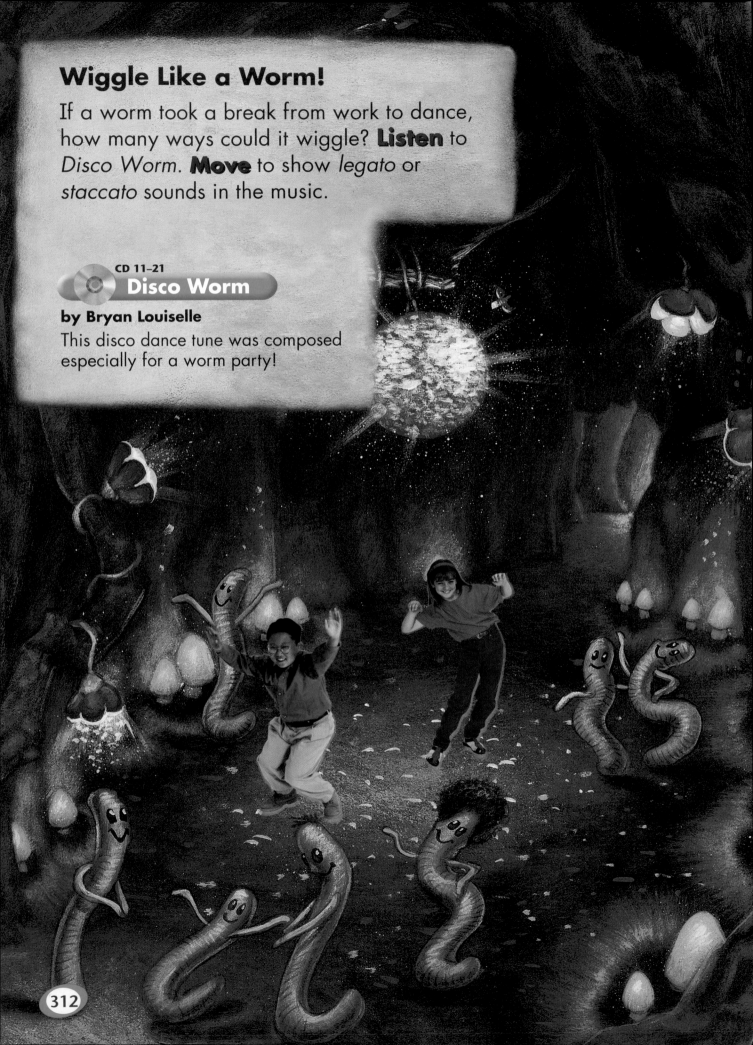

Wiggle Like a Worm!

If a worm took a break from work to dance, how many ways could it wiggle? **Listen** to *Disco Worm*. **Move** to show *legato* or *staccato* sounds in the music.

CD 11–21
Disco Worm

by Bryan Louiselle
This disco dance tune was composed especially for a worm party!

312

As the Worm Turns

Write a play about what happens after this worm meeting. Use your "worm moves" and the song "Lots of Worms" in your play.

The Worms March

In your play, **perform** these ostinatos about ways worms help the planet.

For - ward   wig-gle for - ward   wig-gle

Gar-bage yum!   Gar-bage yum!

Aer-ate   the   soil,   clean up   the Earth!

PLUCKIN' PATTERNS

A catfish has patterns of whiskers. This song has rhythm patterns for you to find. **Listen** for the patterns as you **sing** the song.

CD 11–22

BANJO SAM

Folk Song from North Carolina

do

F

1. Cat - fish, cat - fish, go - in' up - stream,

C   F

Cat - fish, cat - fish where you been?

F

I grabbed . that cat - fish by ___ the snout,

C   F

I pulled _ that cat - fish wrong - side out.

F   C   F

Yo - ho! _____ Ban - jo Sam!

2. As I was goin' through the field,
A black snake bit me on the heel.
I grabbed a stick and done my best,
And ran my head in a hornet's nest.
Yo-ho! Banjo Sam!

3. As I was goin' down the road,
I met a terrapin and a toad.
The terrapin, he began to sing,
The toad, he cut the pigeon-wing.
Yo-ho! Banjo Sam!

Finding the Pattern

How many times can you find this pattern in the song?

You can **perform** the pattern in these ways. First **clap** it. Then **pat** it on your body.

Now choose a part and **perform** this speech piece.

1.   Cat - fish where you been? Cat - fish where you been?

2.   You cat - fish, you.   You cat - fish, you.

Listen to this traditional banjo music.

CD 11–24

Rumblin' On

by Roger McGuinn

This song is from the Ozark mountains.

Arts Connection

◄ *The Banjo Lesson* by Henry Ossawa Tanner, 1893, Oil on canvas.

It's Your Planet

You can help keep the Earth clean. One thing you can do is be sure to recycle whenever you can.

Recycled Music

You can make music with stuff other people think is trash. to 3+2 for some ideas. What do you think is making the sounds?

CD 11–25
3+2
by Donald Knaack

3+2 is from a collection of pieces written for and performed on recycled materials and everyday objects.

Our Planet Earth

The Earth is our home.
We must learn respect
for the many beauties
of our planet. We must
also keep Earth healthy.

Keep It Clean

Sing this song about some ways to keep Earth healthy.

CD 11–26

Don't Dump Trash!

Words and Music by Jill Jarboe

1. Don't dump trash on the ground.

Don't dump trash on the ground.

It hurts the flow'rs and the trees, and it will

hurt you and me. _____

So don't dump trash on the ground.

2. Don't dump trash in the sea.
   Don't dump trash in the sea.
   It hurts the fish and the whales
      from their fins down to their tails.
   So don't dump trash in the sea.

3. Don't dump trash in the air.
   Don't dump trash in the air.
   All the birds want to fly
      through a pretty clean sky.
   So don't dump trash in the air.

4. Don't dump trash on the moon.
   Don't dump trash on the moon.
   It fills the craters and the cracks
      on the front and on the back.
   So don't dump trash on the moon.

5. Don't dump trash anywhere.
   Don't dump trash anywhere.
   Except in the dump,
      where it's all in a lump.
   No, don't dump trash anywhere.

318

Earth Sounds

Read aloud the poem "Breaks Free."
Create sounds to accompany the poem.

Breaks Free

by Frank Asch

I just want to be
where the earth breaks free
of concrete and metal and glass,
of asphalt and plastic and gas,
where sun is king
and water is queen,
where cactus grows tall
and the air is clean.
I just want to be
where the earth breaks free
of fences and alleys and walls,
of factories and traffic and malls,
where owls sleep
in the heart of day
waiting for sunset
to hunt their prey,
where mountains rise
in seas of sand
and coyotes roam
across the land.

A New Day

Each day gives us a new opportunity to care for and enjoy our planet. Music is a great way to start each day.

Sing this good morning song!

CD 11–28 **Every Morning When I Wake Up**

Words and Music by Avon Gillespie

do-

Ev - e - ry morn - ing when I wake _ up

I have a new song to sing, my chil - dren,

Ev - e - ry morn - ing when I wake _ up

I have a new song to sing.

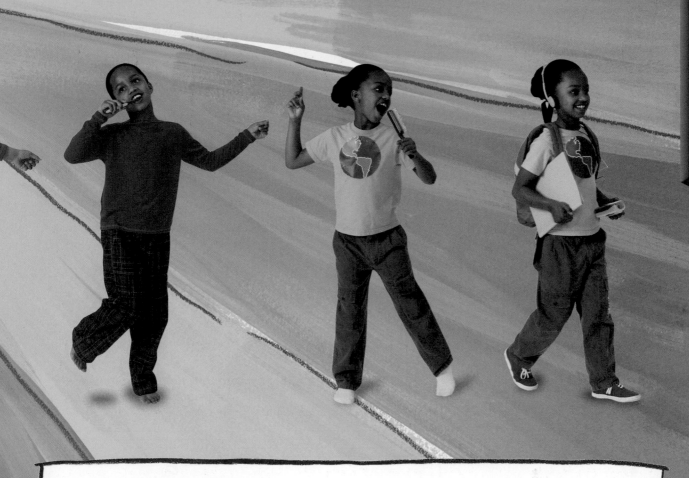

Morning Music

Play these ostinatos to accompany "Every Morning When I Wake Up."

Sing for the Trees

We need trees. The red cedar tree is very important to the Lummi people of Washington State. It is used for carving the great totem poles.

Sing this song about the cedar tree. On the last note of the song, sing softer and softer.

Tall Cedar Tree

CD 11–30

Words and Music by Joseph Hillaire, Lummi Elder
As sung by Pauline Hillaire

Tall _____ ce - dar tree,

1. clap your hands and sing to me. ____
2. clap your hands and dance with me. ____
3. clap your hands and play with me. ____

Wey he yoh, wey he he yoh,

wey he yoh ___ wey he he yoh. ___

Song for the Earth

Listen to this Navajo song about the importance of rain for all living things.

CD 11–32
The Rain Song

by Sharon Burch

This song was written during a drought in 1988.

MUSIC MAKERS

Sharon Burch

Sharon Burch (born 1959) is a Grammy Award-winning singer and songwriter. Her mother is Navajo and her father is German. She says, "Having a German father and a Native mother helped me understand that a human can relate to all people . . . The whole planet is ours; there should be no boundaries."

Music of the

The wind swirls all over the planet. It creates the energy that makes sailboats sail, kites fly, and windmills turn, but we cannot see it. How do we know it's there?

Sing this song about how the wind moves through trees.

CD 11–33

Who Has Seen the Wind?

Words by Christina Rossetti

Melody from Zion's Harp

1. Who   has   seen   the   wind? _____
2. Who   has   seen   the   wind? _____

Nei - ther   I   nor _____ you!
Nei - ther   you   nor _____ I:

Wind

Move Like the Wind

Find the phrases in "Who Has Seen the Wind?"
Move to show each phrase as you **sing** the song.
Stretch your arms in wide curves and feel the wind.

But when the leaves hang trem - bling
But when the trees bow down _ their heads

The wind is pass - ing through,
The wind is pass - ing by.

The wind is pass - ing ___ through.
The wind is pass - ing ___ by.

Wind in Music

Listen to *Epilogue*, music about the cold wind of the Antarctic. Close your eyes and imagine the wind howling.

CD 11–35

Epilogue

from *Sinfonia Antarctica*
by Ralph Vaughan Williams
The wind sounds in this piece were created by a special device called a wind machine.

To a Red Kite

by Lilian Moore

Fling
yourself
upon the sky.

Take the string
you need.
Ride high,

high
above the park.
Tug and buck
and lark
with the wind.

Touch a cloud,
red kite.
Follow the wild geese
in their flight.

Tune In

Ben Franklin discovered electricity while flying a kite.

326

Fun with the Wind!

Flying kites in the wind is fun. Pretend your hand is a kite. Let your "kite hand" lead you.

CD 11–36

Let's Go Fly a Kite

Words and Music by Richard M. Sherman and Robert B. Sherman

Let's   go   fly   a   kite   Up   to   the   high - est height!

Let's   go   fly   a   kite   And send   it   soar - ing

Up   through the   at - mos-phere,   Up   where the   air   is   clear.

Oh,   let's   go ____ fly   a   kite! _____

CD-ROM Use *Making Music* software to create some "wind" music. Experiment with high and low sounds.

Move with the Rain

Water is something our planet cannot live without. Rain is one way we get water. **Sing** this song about fun things to do on a rainy day. **Sing** *staccato* on the words *drip, drop.*

CD 12–1

Falling Rain

Words by Susan Marcus | *Music by April Kassirer*

REFRAIN

G₇ ... C

I can hear the fall - ing rain,

G₇ ... C G Am

Think I'm gon - na stay in - side to - day,

G₇ ... C G Am C

Think I'm gon - na stay in - side and play and

Dm ... G ... C ... *To Coda after verse 3*

lis - ten to the fall - ing rain.

After the Rain

What happens to rain after it falls to the Earth? **Move** to show rain falling from clouds, flowing back to the oceans, then evaporating to become clouds and rain again.

VERSE

1. Drip, drop, drip, drop, Well, I'll pile my pil - lows way up high, _ And make a rock - et ship for me to fly, _ And

D. C. al Coda

you can come,_ there's room for _three, And we'll be back_for tea. _

⊕ CODA

Drip, drop, drip, drop, And lis-ten to the fall - ing rain.

2. Drip, drop, drip, drop,
   A box will be my TV screen,
   I'll be a monster with my face all green,
   And in a monster voice you'll hear
       me say,
   "Buy monster's soup today." *Refrain*

3. Drip, drop, drip, drop,
   I'll fill my bathtub to the brim,
   And when it's full I'll climb right in,
   I'll keep my clothes on just in case
   I have to go someplace.
   Refrain and Coda

Dance a Wonderful Day!

Plants, animals, and people need the sun to live. The sun warms and lights our planet. Think of a bright, sunny day. **Move** to show how it makes you feel.

CD 12–4

Zip-a-Dee-Doo-Dah

Words by Ray Gilbert

Music by Allie Wrubel

Zip - a-dee-doo - dah, zip - a-dee - ay, ___

my, oh my, ___ what a won-der-ful day! ___

Plen - ty of sun - shine, head - in' my way, ___

Zip - a-dee - doo - dah, zip - a-dee - ay! ___

Zip-a-Dee-Dance!

Skip around the room as you **sing** the **A** section of "Zip-a-Dee-Doo-Dah." During the **B** section, stand still and only move your arms.

Mis-ter Blue-bird on my shoul-der, ____

it's the truth   it's "act-ch'll,"   ev-'ry-thing is "sat-is-fact-ch'll."

Zip - a-dee-doo - dah,   zip - a-dee - ay! ___

Won - der-ful   feel - ing,   won-der-ful   day. ___

Sing a Rainbow!

Sometimes, after it rains, you can see something special in the sky. It is very colorful. What is it?

Sing this song about a rainbow.

CD 12–6

The Rainbow

Children's Song from the United States

1. Af - ter the rain is the rain - bow,

Af - ter the rain, then the sun comes out a - gain;

Af - ter the rain is the rain - bow,

Pret - ty rain - bow in the sky.

2. Red, yellow, blue is the rainbow,
   Orange and green
     and a lovely violet;
   Painting the sky is the rainbow,
   Pretty rainbow in the sky.

3. Rainbows are telling a story,
   Rainbows are saying
     the sun comes out again;
   After the rain is the rainbow,
   Pretty rainbow in the sky.

Rainbow Phrases

Sing this phrase.

Where do you find this phrase in "The Rainbow"? **Create** a movement for it. Each time you sing the phrase, **perform** your movement.

A Louisiana Rainbow

Listen to this Cajun-style song from Louisiana.

CD 12–8

L'arc en ciel

by Sharon Arms Doucet

In English, the French title *L'arc en ciel* means "the arch in the sky." What do you think the song is about?

Play into the Sunset

At the end of the day, you can watch a beautiful sunset. As the light fades into a night sky, what do you see?

Play one of these rhythm patterns as you **listen** to *"En nuestra Tierra tan linda."*

Arts Connection

Sunsets (1956) by Diego Rivera. He painted twenty sunsets in Acapulco, Mexico. ▶

Sky Sounds

Now **sing** this song about the beauty
of our planet Earth.

CD 12–9
MIDI 23

En nuestra Tierra tan linda

Words and Music by José-Luis Orozco

1. En nues - tra Tie - rra tan lin - da _____

pron - to va a sa - lir el sol, _____

pron - to va a sa - lir el sol _____

en nues - tra Tie - rra tan lin - da. _____

2. En nuestra Tierra tan linda
   pronto va a salir la luna,
   pronto va a salir la luna
   en nuestra Tierra tan linda.

3. En nuestra Tierra tan linda
   pronto brillará una estrella,
   pronto brillará una estrella
   en nuestra Tierra tan linda.

Star Textures

Have you ever made a wish upon a star? What did you wish for?

The Star Festival is a special day in Japan. Children make wishes and tie them to a tree branch. They believe that the stars will grant their wishes and help them improve their writing skills.

CD 12–12

Tanabata - sama
(Star Festival)

Words by Hanayo Gondo with Ryuha Hayashi
English Words by Mary Shamrock

Music by Kan-ichi Shimofusa
School Song from Japan

1. さ　さ　の　は　さ　ら　さ　ら
1. Sa - sa　no　ha　sa - ra　sa - ra,
1. In　the　sky　the　stars　twin - kle　bright;

の　き　ば　に　ゆ　れ　る
No - ki - ba　ni　yu - re - ru,
Bam - boo　rust - ling　in　the　night.

Starry Sounds

Play these patterns with *"Tanabata-sama"* as the class sings the song. **Describe** the texture. Is it thin or thick?

お ほ し さ ま き ら き ら
O - ho - shi sa - ma ki - ra ki - ra
Glit - ter - ing sparks of sil - ver and gold

き ん ぎ ん す な ご
Ki - n gi - n su - na - go.
High a - bove us we be - hold.

2. *Goshiki no tanzaku,*
   Watashi ga kaita,
   Ohoshi sama kira kira,
   Sora kara miteru.

2. Choose your fondest wishes to write
   On the strips of paper bright.
   Then tie your wishes high on the tree;
   Stars will grant them, you will see.

Star Gazing

 Listen to the changing textures in *Sous les étoiles*.

CD 12–16

Sous les étoiles

from *Les Rêves de Columbine*, Op. 65 by Amy Beach

Sous les étoiles means "under the stars" in French.

M·U·S·I·C M·A·K·E·R·S

Amy Beach

Amy Beach (1867–1944) was a child prodigy. She was composing and playing the piano when she was only four years old. Beach grew up to become the best-known American woman composer of her time. She played the piano for concerts in the United States and Europe. Her music was played by some of the most famous orchestras in the world.

 Listen to the changing textures in *Gavotte* as you follow the listening map.

CD 12–17

Gavotte

from *Symphony No. 1 in D Major*, Op. 25 ("Classical") by Sergei Prokofiev

The gavotte is a lively dance that comes from France.

Second time only

Music for a Comet

Halley Came to Jackson is the story of someone who was alive for two visits by Halley's comet.

Tune In

Halley's comet appeared in 1910, then again in 1986. How many years were in between appearances?

Listen to the song and learn when the comet visited. What instruments do you hear on the recording?

CD 12–18
Halley Came to Jackson

by Mary Chapin Carpenter
Carpenter was inspired to write this song after reading the story by Eudora Welty.

M·U·S·I·C M·A·K·E·R·S

Mary Chapin Carpenter

Mary Chapin Carpenter (born 1958) is a singer-songwriter from Princeton, New Jersey. She has won many awards for her songs and recordings. She is active in organizations that are committed to making a better world for everyone.

Care for the Ocean

Sing this song about the danger of littering in our oceans. **Describe** the form of the song.

CD 12–19 ## From Sea to Shining Sea

Words and Music by Gene Grier and Lowell Everson

VERSE

E♭

1. Oil   and   wa - ter,   they   just   don't   mix;
2. Su - per   tank - er   crashed   on   a   reef;
3. Oil   and   wa - ter,   they   just   don't   mix;

A♭   E♭

that's   a   guar - an - tee.
was - n't   meant ___ to   be.
that's   a   guar - an - tee.

E♭

Fish   and   wild - life   get   ver - y   sick
Beach - es   cov - ered   with   oil   and   grease
Fish   and   wild - life   get   ver - y   sick

3rd time to Coda ⊕

A♭

from   sea   to   shin - ing   sea.
from   sea   to   shin - ing   sea.
from   sea   to   shin - ing   sea.

Save the Sea Creatures

If we are careful to keep the waters clean, our fishy friends will survive.

Create more verses about keeping the oceans clean. **Sing** your new verses.

REFRAIN

From sea to shin - ing sea,

on this we will ___ a - gree.

To keep the wa - ter free

from ref - use and ___ de - bris.

Coda

From sea to shin - ing sea, from sea to shin - ing sea.

The Oceans of the Earth

Most of the Earth's surface is covered by oceans. Weather affects the seas in many ways. **Listen** to this song from Spain and decide what type of weather it suggests.

Sounds of the Sea

Create your own **introduction** and coda using sea sounds. Then **sing** the song with the introduction and coda that you created.

An **introduction** is a short section placed at the beginning of a song.

CD 12–21

La mar estaba serena
(The Sea is Calm)

English Words by Bob Demmert

Folk Song from Spain

La mar es - ta - ba se - re - na,
The sea is peace - ful and calm now,

se - re - na es - ta - ba la mar.
the sea is qui - et and still.

La mar es - ta - ba se - re - na,
The sea is peace - ful and calm ____ now,

se - re - na es - ta - ba la mar.
the sea is qui - et and still.

Sing a Story

Sing this song about the stories you can find in music.

Sing Me a Story

CD 12–25

Words and Music by Jill Gallina

Sing me a sto - ry, a sto - ry in song.

So man - y sto - ries to tell.

Sing me a sto - ry, a sto - ry in song,

'cause mu - sic tells sto - ries so well.

Perform a Story

Music can tell stories in many ways.

Sto-ries with fea - tures of ma-gi-cal crea - tures,

or jour-neys that take __ us a - long. __

Tall tales, or small _ tales, but the best of all __ tales,

are tales that are told __ with a song.

A Musical Story

Solomon is a musical story about King Solomon of Israel. Sheba was the Queen of Ethiopia who came to visit him. *The Arrival of the Queen of Sheba* is music written for her arrival in the king's court. **Listen** to how the timbre of the music changes.

CD 12–27

The Arrival of the Queen of Sheba

from *Solomon*
by George Frideric Handel
as performed by the English Chamber Orchestra

Handel composed the music for this story when he was working in England during the reign of King George I.

MUSIC MAKERS

George Frideric Handel

George Frideric Handel (1685-1759) was born in Germany. He was a fine organist and harpsichordist, and one of the greatest composers of his time. He learned to compose music by writing down the works of other composers. He spent most of his life living and working in England.

The Arrival of the Queen of Sheba
Listening Map

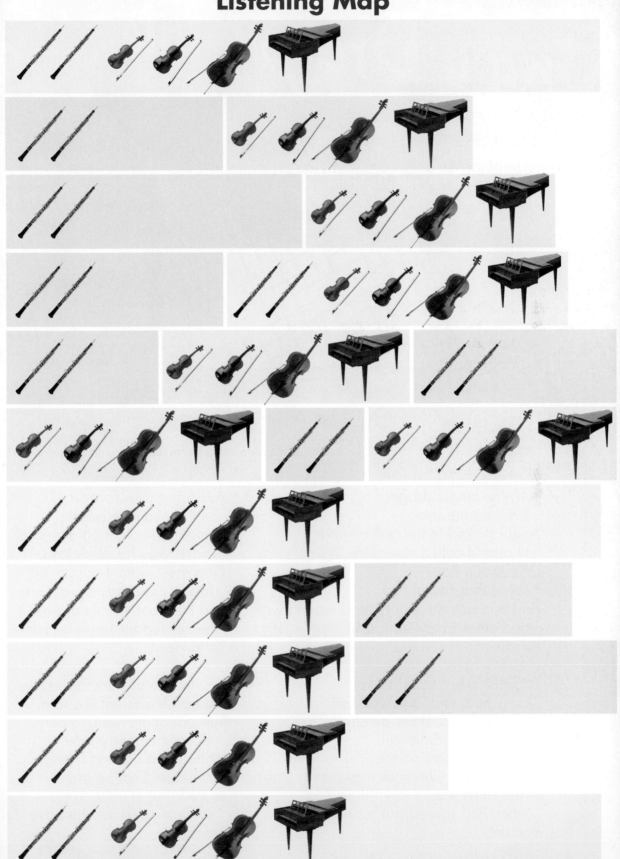

Sing a Dragon Tale

Sing this song that tells the story of Puff, the magic dragon, and his friend. What is the form of the song?

CD 12–28

Puff, the Magic Dragon

Words and Music by Peter Yarrow and Leonard Lipton

VERSE

1. Puff, the magic dragon,
   lived by the sea
   And frolicked in the autumn mist
   in a land called Honahlee.
   Little Jackie Paper
   loved that rascal Puff
   And brought him strings and sealing wax
   and other fancy stuff. Oh!
   Refrain

2. Together they would travel
   on a boat with billowed sail;
   Jackie kept a lookout perched
   on Puff's gigantic tail.
   Noble kings and princes
   would bow whene'er they came;
   Pirate ships would low'r their flag
   when Puff roared out his name. Oh!
   Refrain

3. A dragon lives forever
   but not so little boys;
   Painted wings and giant rings
   make way for other toys.
   One grey night it happened,
   Jackie Paper came no more,
   and Puff that mighty dragon,
   he ceased his fearless roar.
   To Verse 4

4. His head was bent in sorrow;
   green scales fell like rain.
   Puff no longer went to play
   along the cherry lane.
   Without his lifelong friend,
   Puff could not be brave,
   so Puff that mighty dragon
   sadly slipped into his cave. Oh!
   Refrain

Jabuti's Song SAVES THE DAY

Kibungo is the meanest, scariest beast of the Amazon rain forest. **Listen** to the story and follow along with the pictures.

CD 13–1
Kibungo, Beast of the Forest

Now you can **perform** the Kibungo story
with your class.

Songs for a Story

Sing these songs that go with the story of *Kibungo, Beast of the Forest.*

The first song is Kibungo's theme song.

CD 13–2

KIBUNGO

Story-Song from the Amazon Rainforest

Ki - bun - go   o - i   bi - cho do   ma - to.
Ki - bun - go, oh - oh,   beast of   the for - est.

Ki - bun - go   o - i   bi - cho do   ma - to.
Ki - bun - go, oh - oh,   beast of   the for - est.

Jabuti uses this song to trick Kibungo.
Move to show the form of the song.

CD 13–6

O PIÃO ENTROU
(The Top Joined the Circle)

English Words by C. P. Language Institute

Game Song from Brazil

VERSE

O pi - ão en - trou na ro - da ó pi - ão
Oh, the top joined in the cir - cle to spin.

O pi - ão en - trou na ro - da ó pi - ão,
Oh, the top joined in the cir - cle to spin.

REFRAIN

Ro - da ó pi - ão bam - bei - a pi - ão,
Spin, __ spin, the top, oh, spin, whirl - ing top.

Ro - da ó pi - ão bam - bei - a pi - ão.
Spin, ___ spin, the top, oh, spin, whirl - ing top.

2. Sapateia no terreiro
   ó pião, (Repeat)
   Refrain

3. Pega a mão do teo parceiro
   ó pião, (Repeat)
   Refrain

2. Tap away in the clearing,
   dance, spinning top. (Repeat)
   Refrain

3. Take your partner by the hand,
   spinning top. (Repeat)
   Refrain

Perform a Story

Sing a Legend

Sometimes people use songs to tell a story about their beliefs. Sing this song from the Pima people of Arizona. It tells how they believe Earth began. Move to show the direction of the melody.

Chuhwuht

CD 13–12

Native American Song of the Pima as sung by Chief Visak-Vo-o-yim

Chuh - wuht - tah   ma - ka - i,   chuh - wuht - tuh   na - to.

Chuh-wuht - tuh   ma - ka - i,   chuh-wuht - tuh   na - to.

Hi - ma - lo,   hi - ma - lo,

Hi - ma - lo,   hi - ma - cho!

Story in a Poem

Songs and poems tell stories in their own ways. This poem is from the Wintu people of California. It is part of their story about the beginning of the world.

Perform a Story

The Stars Streaming in the Sky

Traditional Wintu

The stars streaming in
the sky are my hair.
The round rim of the
Earth which you see
Binds my starry hair.

SOUNDS OF A TRAIN

Before airplanes were invented, trains were the speediest form of travel.

Listen to the accompaniment of this railroad song. **Describe** the sounds you hear.

CD 13–15
MIDI 24

She'll Be Comin' 'Round the Mountain

Railroad Song

1. She'll be com - in' round the moun - tain when she
2. She'll be driv - in' six white hor - ses when she

comes, (toot, toot!) She'll be com - in' round the moun-tain when she
comes, (chug, chug!) She'll be driv - in' six white hor - ses when she

comes, (toot, toot!) She'll be com - in' round the
comes, (chug, chug!) She'll be driv - in' six white

Creating Train Sounds

Create your own special sound effects to accompany the song. Make them sound like a train.

moun-tain, She'll be com-in' round the moun-tain, She'll be
hor-ses, She'll be driv-in' six white hor-ses, She'll be

com-in' round the moun-tain when she comes. (toot, toot!)
driv-in' six white hor-ses when she comes. (chug, chug!)

3. Oh, we'll all have chicken and dumplings when she comes, (yum, yum!) . . .

4. Oh, we'll all go out to meet her when she comes, (Hi, there!) . . .

A Song that Grows!

Create movements to help you remember the verses of this song. A song that keeps growing is called a **cumulative song.** Do you know other songs like this?

A **cumulative song** gets longer as each new verse is added.

CD 13–17

The Tree in the Wood

Traditional Cumulative Song from England

VERSE

1. All in ___ a ___ wood there grew a tree,
2. Now on ___ this ___ tree there grew a limb,

The fi - nest ___ tree you ev - er did see.
The fi - nest ___ limb you ev - er did see.

Repeat as necessary

The tree was in the ground,
The limb was on the tree,

Tell Your Own Story

Write a cumulative story with a partner.
Then **create** sound effects to accompany
your story.

REFRAIN

and the green grass grew all a-round a-round a-round

and the green grass grew all a-round.

3. Now on this limb there grew a branch,
   The finest branch you ever did see.
   The branch was on the limb,
   The limb was on the tree,
   The tree was in the ground,
   Refrain

4. Now on this branch there was a bough, . . . *Refrain*

5. Now on this bough there was a twig, . . . *Refrain*

6. And on this twig there was a leaf, . . . *Refrain*

7. And by this leaf there was a nest, . . . *Refrain*

8. And in this nest there was an egg, . . . *Refrain*

9. And in this egg there was a bird, . . . *Refrain*

10. And on this bird there was a wing, . . . *Refrain*

11. And on this wing there was a feather, . . . *Refrain*

12. And on this feather there was a flea, . . . *Refrain*

Sing a Funny Story

Music and poetry often tell stories just for fun. **Sing** the story of "The Crocodile." Then read the poem.

CD 13–19

The Crocodile

Traditional

She sailed a - way on a love - ly sum - mer day
on the back of a croc - o - dile;
"You'll see," said she, "he's as tame as tame can be,
I'll ride him down the Nile."

How Doth the Little Crocodile
by Lewis Carroll

How doth the little crocodile
Improve his shining tail,
And pour the waters of the Nile
On every golden scale!
How cheerfully he seems to grin,
How neatly spreads his claws,
And welcomes little fishes in
With gently smiling jaws!

Melody Patterns

Find repeated patterns in the melody of
"The Crocodile."

The croc winked his eye as she bade them all good-bye,

wear - ing a hap - py smile;

At the end of the ride the lad - y was in - side

and the smile was on the croc - o - dile! Yum Yum!

Cajun Crocodile Song

The Cajuns are people in Louisiana whose ancestors were French. Here is a Cajun song about two crocodiles. **Listen** for the same and different phrases in the song.

 CD 13–21

Deux cocodries
(Two Crocodiles)

English Words by Edith Bicknell

Cajun Singing Game from Louisiana

Deux co-co-dries sont al-lés à la guer-re,
Two croc-o-diles were go-ing off to war, ___

dis-ant "a-dieu" à leurs pe-tits en-fants. ___
Say-ing "so long!" as they went out the door. ___

Leurs lon-gues queues traîn-aient dans la pous-sièr-e,
Long tails be-hind, through mud they did ad-vance, ___

ils sont al-lés com-battre les é-lé-phants. _
Ea-ger to fight their foes the el-e-phants. _

364

Si les co - co - dries, les co - co - dries, les co - co - dries ___
If the croc - o - diles, the croc - o - diles, the croc - o - diles ___

sur le bord d'ba-you se sont per - dus, n'en par-lons plus, ___
lose their way a - long the ba - you, then our sto-ry's through, -

Si les co - co - dries, les co - co - dries, les co - co - dries ___
If the croc - o - diles, the croc - o - diles, the croc - o - diles ___

sur le bord d'ba-you se sont per - dus, n'en par-lons plus. ___
lose their way a - long the ba - you, then our sto-ry's through. -

Dancing Animals

You are invited to an animal dance! Which animal would you like to be? **Sing** the story "Jig Along Home."

CD 13–25

Jig Along Home

Words and Music by Woody Guthrie

VERSE · F · C₇

1. I went to the dance and the an - i - mals came;
2. ⁊ Fishing worm — danced the — fish - ing — reel;

C₇ · F

The jay - bird danced with horse - shoes on.
⁊ Lob - ster danced on the pea - cock's tail.

F · B♭

The grass - hop - per danced till he fell on the floor!
⁊ Ba - boon — danced with the ris - ing — moon.

F · C₇ · F

Jig a - long, jig a - long, jig a - long home.
Jig a - long, jig a - long, jig a - long home.

Your Own Dance Moves

Create your own movements for each animal.
How will you **move** during the refrain?

Perform a Story

REFRAIN

Jig, jig - a jig, jig - a jig a - long home,

Jig, jig - a jig, jig - a jig a - long home.

Jig a - long, jig a - long, jig a - long home.

Jig, jig - a jig, jig - a jig a - long home.

3. Mama rat took off her hat,
   Shook the house with the old tom cat.
   The alligator beat his tail on the drum,
   Jig along, jig along, jig along home.
   Refrain

4. The boards did rattle and the house
      did shake;
   The clouds did laugh and the world
      did quake.
   New moon rattled some silver spoons,
   Jig along, jig along, jig along home.
   Refrain

5. The nails flew loose and the floors
      broke down;
   Everybody danced around and
      around.
   The house came down and the
      crowd went home,
   Jig along, jig along, jig along home.
   Refrain

A Story with a Moral

Listen to a song that tells a famous story. What is the moral, or lesson, of the story?

CD 13–27
Yertle the Turtle

by The Red Hot Chili Peppers

This popular group wrote the song, *Yertle the Turtle*, based on the story by Dr. Seuss.

Create Story Music

Create your own music to go with a story you like. Follow these steps.

1. Form a group of four or five people.
2. Choose a story.
3. Decide what instruments you want to use.

Remember, you can
- Create a rhythm.
- Invent a melody.
- Play an ostinato.

Perform your story and music for the class.

A Climbing Song

Have you ever been the first in line? How did you get there? **Sing** this song about taking care of others as you climb the ladder of success.

Words and Music by Bryan Louiselle

CD 13–28

Look Out Below!

You might be a ver - y good climb - er

But no mat - ter how high you go,

Take the time, make the time

To look af - ter those be - low.

Melody with Steps

Sing the song again. How does the melody climb upward?

'Cause ta - bles can turn in a min - ute

And all of your climb - ing might stop,

And folks you'd as - signed to stay be - hind

Could sud - den - ly wind up on top.

Sing to Celebrate

Here is a song you can sing for any special occasion.

CD 13–30

It's a Celebration!

Words and Music by Katherine Dines

We are smil - ing in the sun

As the sea - sons go and come.

Fam - i - lies _____ a - round the world

Wel - come ev - 'ry boy and girl.

It's a cel - e - bra - tion, _ a cel - e - bra - tion,

It's a cel - e - bra - tion, _ a cel - e - bra - tion. _

Celebrate the Season

People around the world celebrate in many ways throughout the year. What special days do you celebrate with your family?

Fiesta Time!

Fiestas are big parties where people celebrate with singing and dancing. This song is written in a style called *huayno*. Let's go to the fiesta!

Vamos a la fiesta
(Let's Go to the Party)

CD 14–1

Words and Music by Juanita Newland-Ulloa
From Canta Conmigo, Vol. 2

Va - mos a la fies - ta la fies - ta la fies - ta
Let's go to the par - ty, the par - ty, the par - ty

Va - mos a la fies - ta a go - zar
Let's go to the par - ty, we'll have fun.

To - dos los ni - ñi - tos muy chi - qui - ti - tos.
All the lit - tle chil - dren, they'll all be danc - ing.

To - dos los ni - ñi - tos a bai - lar.
All the lit - tle chil - dren, they will sing.

Fiesta Percussion

Play these rhythm patterns to accompany
"Vamos a la fiesta."

Now **improvise** your own rhythm patterns
while the class sings the song.

OOOOooh! It's Halloween!

Here is a spooky song for Halloween. **Sing** "Skin and Bones." Use dynamics to express the mood of the song. How will you sing *BOO!* in the song?

 CD 14–5

Skin and Bones

Folk Song from Kentucky

1. There was an old wo - man all skin and bones,
2. She lived — down by — the old grave-yard,

Oo - oo - oo - ooh! — 7. She op-ened the door and BOO!

3. One night she thought she'd take a walk, . . .
4. She walked down by the old graveyard, . . .
5. She saw the bones a-lyin' around, . . .
6. She went to the closet to get a broom, . . .

A Halloween Chat

An owl and a pumpkin have a friendly chat in the song on the next page. Use your voice to show the two characters.

The Owl and the Pumpkin

Words by Betty Barlow and Victoria Shima

Music by Betty Barlow

An owl in the tree looked down be-low and winked his eye.

"Who are you? Who are you?"

A pump-kin on the ground looked up and gave a friend-ly shout:

"Yoo - hoo! Yoo - hoo!"

The full moon said that they should get to - geth - er.

So now you'll hear in ev - 'ry kind of weath - er:

"Who are yoo - hoo! Who are yoo - hoo!

Who are yoo - hoo!"

Harvest Time

"*Perot*" is a song for the Jewish harvest holiday called *Sukkot*. As you **sing** the song, **move** to show the phrases.

CD 14–9

Perot
(Fruit)

English Words by David Eddleman   *Traditional Song for Sukkot*

do

Pe - rot,   pe - rot!
Buy   fruit!   Buy   fruit!

Mi ro - tzeh lik - not   Pe - rot le - chag Suk - kot?
Who will buy my fruit   to ce - le - brate Suk - kot?

A - na - vim ve - ta - pu - chim, a - na - vim ve - ta - pu - chim,
In the *suk - kah* you will dine, Grapes and ap - ples, oh, so fine;

Ve - ag - va - ni - yah   lit - lot al gag Suk - kah.
Plump to - ma - toes, too,   are hang - ing there for you.

A *Sukkot* Tradition

Sukkot is celebrated in the fall and lasts nine days. One of the traditions is to build a *sukkah,* or tent, by the house and decorate it with flowers, fruits, and vegetables.

Celebrate Thanksgiving

Many people celebrate a Thanksgiving holiday.
Often people gather with friends and family for a
holiday meal.

Here is a Thanksgiving song for you to **sing**.

 CD 14–13

Thanksgiving Is Near

Words and Music by Grace Nash

1. Oc - to - ber   is   o - ver, Thanks-giv - ing   is   near.

Can't you   smell tur - key   and stuff - ing   right here?

And when it   is   o - ver   and thanks have   been said,

it   won't be   the   tur - key   but   me stuffed   in - stead!

2. The Thanksgiving table is loaded with treats.
It's hard to use caution and not overeat.
But when it is over and I'm stuffed in bed,
I'll wish that the turkey had gobbled instead.

A Thanksgiving Poem

Listen to this poem. Then **create** a rhythm pattern to accompany the poem.

Setting the Thanksgiving Table
by X. J. Kennedy

Fetch bouquets of bittersweet.
Give them to wild birds to eat.

Bring the homely freckled gourd.
Let it ornament our board.

Bring the pumpkin plump in shape,
Bring the perfect purple grape.

Pile the polished apples high,
Granny Smith and Northern Spy,

Bring the chestnut in its fur
Coat of bristly brownish burr,

Bring in sun-bleached stalks, each ear
Ripe and golden as the year.

Bring, each day you wake and live,
Fresh supplies of thanks to give.

CHANUKAH
The Festival of Lights

Chanukah is a Jewish holiday. It is usually celebrated in December. Every night for eight nights, a candle is lit in a special candleholder. This candleholder is called a *menorah*.

Here is a song you can **sing** to celebrate Chanukah.

Chanukah Is Here!

CD 14–15

Words and Music by Judith Eisenstein and Frieda Prensky

Flick-er lit-tle can-dles; flick-er bright for Cha-nu-kah.

Se-vi-von go spin-ning round and round on Cha-nu-kah.

Flick-er lit-tle can-dles, all eight nights of Cha-nu-kah.

Se-vi-von go spin-ning, Cha-nu-kah is here!

Another Chanukah Song

"*Ner li*" is another Chanukah song that you can sing. **Describe** the form of this song.

Mmm. I like my *latkes* with sour cream!

Tune In

Latkes are one of the favorite foods eaten at Chanukah time. They are fried crispy potato pancakes.

CD 14–17

Ner li
(The Light)

Words by Levin Kipnis
English Words by David ben Avraham

Music by Mifalei Tarbuth

Ner __ li __ ner li, ner __ li da - kik,
For __ the __ light, the light __ long a - go,

Ba, __ Cha - nu - kah, ne - ri ad - lik,
Let __ us __ set the can - dles a - glow;

Ba, Cha - nu - kah, ne - ri a ir
Come, Cha - nu - kah, where light be - longs,

Ba, Cha - nu - kah, shir - im a - shir.
Come, Cha - nu - kah, we sing your __ songs.

Celebrate Christmas

Christmas is a holiday that celebrates the birth of Jesus. In the United States, Christmas is on December 25. Songs for Christmas are called carols. Here is a German Christmas carol you can **sing**.

CD 14-21

O laufet, ihr Hirten

(Come Running, You Shepherds)

English Words by George K. Evans

Traditional Silesian Carol from Germany

O lau - fet ihr Hir - ten, lauft al - le zu - gleich,
Come run - ning, you shep - herds, as fast _ as you can,

Und neh - men Schal - mei - en und Pfeif - en mit euch!
With flutes and with bag - pipes, and with _ your whole clan.

Lauft _ al - le _ zu - mal mit _ freu - di - gem _ Schall,
We're _ go - ing _ to _ see, In _ Beth - le - hem's _ stall,

Nach Beth - le - hem zum Kripp - lein, zum Kripp - lein im Stall!
The child _ whom the an - gels an - nounced _ to us all.

Santa Is Coming

The story of Santa Claus came to the United States with European immigrants.

Listen to this song about Santa Claus. Then **describe** the direction of the melody.

CD 14–25

It's Santa – Again!

Words and Music by Elizabeth Gilpatrick

1. See the rein-deer tak-ing flight ____
2. Stashed be-hind him 'way in back ____

On a clear De-cem-ber night. ____
I see his e-nor-mous pack. ____

Can you see him flash-ing by,
I have heard it's filled with toys,

Out a-cross the win-ter sky?
For all the girls and all the boys.

You'll miss him if you blink your eye: it's San-ta a-gain!
Hush now, don't you make a noise: it's San-ta a-gain!

A Christmas Waltz

Sometimes it is hard to wait for Christmas. Here is a song about Christmas excitement. It has a long—short rhythm grouped in sets of threes. **Move** to the rhythm and the meter as you **sing** the song.

CD 14–27

Christmas, Don't Be Late
(The Chipmunk Song)

Words and Music by Ross Bagdasarian

Christ - mas, Christ - mas time is near,

Time for toys and time for cheer.

We've been good, but we can't last.

Hur - ry Christ - mas, hur - ry fast.

Moving in 3

Listen to *Les patineurs* (The Skaters) by Emile Waldteufel [VALD-toy-fehl].

What is the meter of the music? Pretend you are an Olympic skater. Skate using long, smooth strokes. Where will you walk on tip-toe and twirl?

CD 14–29

Les patineurs

by Emile Waldteufel as performed by the Rochester Philharmonic Orchestra

This music was written for dancing the Viennese waltz, a smooth, gliding dance in triple meter.

Arts Connection

The Skater, by Gilbert Stuart ▲ (1755–1828).

Want a plane that loops the loop.

Me, I want a hu - la hoop.

We can hard - ly stand the wait. Please

Christ - mas, don't be late.

Winter Fun!

Imagine taking a sleigh ride on a snowy night. What would you see? What kinds of sounds would you hear on a sleigh ride?

Here is a festive song you might **sing** on your sleigh ride.

CD 14–30

Jingle Bells

Words and Music by James Pierpont

VERSE

Dash-ing through the snow,   In a one-horse o - pen sleigh,

O'er the fields we   go,   Laugh-ing   all   the way.

Bells   on Bob - tail   ring,   Mak - ing spir - its bright;   What

fun   it   is   to ride and sing A sleigh-ing song to - night! Oh!

388

Arts **Connection**

▲ *Holiday Sleigh Ride* (1993)
serigraph by Jane Wooster Scott

REFRAIN

Jin - gle bells, jin - gle bells, Jin - gle all the way!

Oh, what fun it is to ride In a one-horse o - pen sleigh! _

Jin - gle bells, jin - gle bells, Jin - gle all the way!

Oh, what fun it is to ride In a one-horse o - pen sleigh!

Going on a Sleigh Ride!

Listen to *Sleigh Ride.* Do you hear something that sounds like a cracking whip? What instrument sounds like a neighing horse at the end?

CD 14–32
Sleigh Ride

by Leroy Anderson

Anderson uses sleigh bells and a slapstick to make this piece really sound like a sleigh ride.

M·U·S·I·C M·A·K·E·R·S
Leroy Anderson

Leroy Anderson (1908–1975) was born in Cambridge, Massachusetts. He composed orchestra music using unusual sounds, such as a typewriter, a ticking clock, and sandpaper.

A Living Snowman?

Listen to *Frosty, the Snowman*. **Move** to show the changing moods in the song.

CD 14–33

Frosty, the Snowman

by Jack Rollins and Steve Nelson

In 1969 this song was the inspiration for a Christmas television special.

Rap and Play

Did you ever make a snowman? This rap song tells you how.

CD 14–34

Mister Snow Rap

Words by Linda Walsh　　　　　　　　　　*Rhythmic Setting by Bob Demmert*

1. I take some snow from off the ground, —
2. I roll the ball back, to and fro, —

And make a snow - ball, hard and round. —
By add - ing flakes, I watch it grow. —

3. Repeat three times
   and stack them high,
   Then add a nose, a mouth, and eyes.

4. My job's complete
   and now I know
   That I've created Mister Snow.

Play these rhythm patterns with "Mister Snow Rap."

CELEBRATE KWANZAA

Kwanzaa is an African American celebration.
It lasts for seven days.

Sing this song to learn about *Kwanzaa*.
Move to show the direction of the melody.

CD 14–36

A KWANZAA CAROL

Words and Music by Reggie Royal

1. We sing of joy and glad-ness   a song of hope and peace.
2. For sev - en days we ga - ther,   rich prin - ci - ples to learn.

A *Kwan-zaa* ce - le - bra-tion   that means so much to   me.
We learn that we have val - ue   and share what we have earned.

From A - fri - ca   so long a - go   a peo-ple came to   see,
We keep a strong com-mun - i - ty   when we stand up and say:

That each one was a part of what I was to   be.
Each per - son is im - por-tant in their way. _____

REFRAIN

F   C₇

Light   the   lights   so   bright,   ce - le - brate,

F   C   F

for   it's   *Kwan-zaa*   time.   We will laugh and   sing   a

F   B♭   C₇   F

joy - ful   song   at   *Kwan* - *zaa*.

Living the Dream

Martin Luther King, Jr. was an important American leader. He dreamed of equality and justice for all people. He worked hard to help make these dreams come true.

Perform this rap to celebrate the life of Martin Luther King, Jr.

CD 14–38

A Kid Like Me

Words and Music by Cathy Fink and Marcy Marxer

There once was a preacher, Martin Luther King,
He worked day and night to hear freedom ring,
From Selma to Montgomery he led the people
In a struggle to create equal rights for all people.
He didn't use violence, no guns or knives.
His message was one that revered our lives.
We remember his speech, "I have a dream."
He did a lot for kids like you and me.

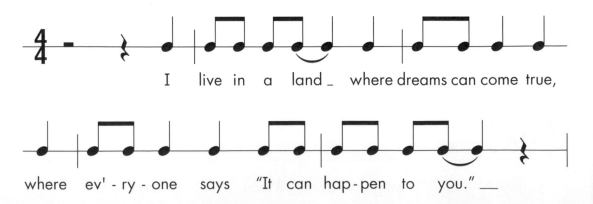

I live in a land _ where dreams can come true,
where ev'-ry-one says "It can hap-pen to you." _

Mar - tin had a dream that he could see, ___

And once up - on a time he was a kid like me. ___

Like me (like you), Like you (like me).

Mar - tin had a dream that he could see, ___

And once up - on a time he was a kid like me. ___

Dreaming of Freedom

Martin Luther King, Jr. gave a famous speech called "I Have a Dream." He ended his speech with words from this spiritual.

CD 14–40

Free at Last

African American Spiritual

REFRAIN

Free at last, ___ free at last, ___

Thank God Al-might-y, I'm free at last, ___

Free at last, ___ free at last, ___

Thank God Al-might-y, I'm free at last. ___

VERSE

1. Way down yonder in the graveyard walk,
   Thank God Almighty, I'm free at last.
   Me and my Jesus gonna meet and talk,
   Thank God Almighty, I'm free at last. *Refrain*

2. On a my knees when the light passed by, . . .
   Thought my soul would rise and fly, . . . *Refrain*

3. Some of these mornings, bright and fair, . . .
   Gonna meet King Jesus in the air, . . . *Refrain*

A Dream of Your Own

Create a call-and-response rap about your dreams. This poem might give you some ideas.

When I Grow Up

by Jack Prelutsky

When I grow up, I think that I
may pilot rockets through the sky,
grow orchards full of apple trees,
or find a way to cure disease.
Perhaps I'll run for president,
design a robot, or invent
unique computerized machines
or miniature submarines.

When I grow up, I'd like to be
the captain of a ship at sea,
an architect, a clown or cook,
the writer of a famous book.
I just might be the one to teach
a chimpanzee the art of speech . . .
but what I'll *really* be, I'll bet
I've not begun to think of yet.

Valentine's Day!

On Valentine's Day people show that they care about their friends and families. They give cards and gifts to one another.

In this Valentine song, you can **sing** about some unusual gifts. What is the form of the song?

CD 14–42

Valentines

Words and Music by Burt Szabo

VERSE

Solo C   G   C

do

1. Don't you send me hearts and flow - ers   if you want to be   my
2. Don't you send me frogs and spi - ders   if you want to be   my

C   G   C   F

val - en - tine,   Send me frogs and   hair - y - leg - ged spi - ders
val - en - tine,   Send me hearts and   choc - o - late __ flow - ers

C   G   C

if   you   want   to   be   my   val - en - tine.
if   you   want   to   be   my   val - en - tine.

398

Send me slugs and bugs and toads, cat - er - pil - lars, ants and
Send me cards with kitty cat smiles, but - ter - fly __ wings and

croc - o - diles, Send me snakes and a worm that squirms,
cud - dly bears, Send me straw - ber - ry tarts and cakes,

and then I'll be your val - en - tine.
and then I'll be your val - en - tine.

REFRAIN
Chorus

Bugs and but - ter -flies live to - geth - er, snakes and frogs and

kit - ty cats, too; All of us can live to - geth - er;

We can all be val - en - tines.

Celebrate SPRING

People in many parts of the world celebrate the arrival of spring. In this folk song from Switzerland, part of the melody sounds like a bird. **Sing** the song, then name the bird.

CD 15–1

L'inverno è passato
(Winter Is Over)

English Words by Edith Bicknell

Folk Song from Switzerland

L'in - ver - no è pas - sa - to, l'a - pri - le non c'è più,
The win - ter now is o - ver, and Ap - ril rains are gone;

è rit - or - na - to il mag - gio al can - to del cu - cù.
It's May a - gain I know for I hear the cuck-oo's song.

Cu - cù, cu - cù, l'a - pri - le non c'è più;
Cuck - oo, cuck - oo, the Ap - ril rains are gone;

è rit - or - na - to il mag - gio al can - to del cu - cù.
It's May a - gain I know for I hear the cuck-oo's song.

Springtime in Japan

In Japan the winters can be very cold. Japanese children sing this song to celebrate the arrival of spring. Move to show the direction of the melody.

CD 15–5
MIDI 25

Haru ga kita
(Springtime Has Come)

Japanese Words by Takano Tatsuyuki
English Words by Patty Zeitlin

School Song from Japan
Music by Okano Teiichi

1. Ha - ru ga ki - ta, ha - ru ga ki - ta
1. Spring - time has come, oh, spring - time has come, oh,

Do - ko _____ ni ki - ta? _____
How do you know it's true? _____

Ya - ma ni ki - ta, Sa - to ni ki - ta,
Look on the moun - tain, Down in the val - ley,

No ni - mo ki - ta. _____
In the prai - rie, too. _____

2. Hana ga saku, hana ga saku,
   Doko ni saku?
   Yama ni saku, Sato ni saku,
   No nimo saku.

2. Flowers are blooming, Flowers are blooming,
   Where are they in bloom?
   Up on the mountain, Down in the valley,
   In the prairie, too.

3. Tori ga naku, tori ga naku,
   Doko de naku,
   Yama de naku, Sato de naku,
   No demo naku.

3. Birds are a-singing, Birds are a-singing,
   Where can we hear them sing?
   Up on the mountain, Down in the valley,
   In the prairie, too.

Celebrate the Season

Celebrate America!

Patriotic songs tell about our country and our freedom. People of all ages sing patriotic songs to show pride in America.

Sing this song. Use dynamics to express the mood of the song.

CD 15–9
MIDI 26

★America, I Hear You Singing ★★

Words and Music by Barberi Paull

1. A - mer - i - ca, I hear you sing-ing,
2. When I sing out your joy - ous an-them,

A - mer - i - ca, your old sweet song;
Yes, ev - 'ry time of you I sing,

Our dreams and hopes, it seems, are borne,
I join your song, A - mer - i - ca,

A - mer - i - ca, in your song. ____
I join in your free - dom song. ____

America Sings!

Singing patriotic songs helps us to understand the people and the history of the United States.

Sing this famous patriotic song about the beauty of our land.

 CD 15–11 **America**

Words by Samuel Francis Smith

Traditional

1. My coun - try! 'tis of thee, Sweet land of lib - er - ty, Of thee I sing; Land where my fa - thers died, Land of the Pil - grims' pride, From ev - 'ry __ moun - tain-side Let __ free - dom ring!

2. My native country, thee,
   Land of the noble free,
   Thy name I love;
   I love thy rocks and rills,
   Thy woods and templed hills;
   My heart with rapture thrills
   Like that above.

3. Let music swell the breeze,
   And ring from all the trees
   Sweet Freedom's song;
   Let mortal tongues awake,
   Let all that breathe partake,
   Let rocks their silence break,
   The sound prolong.

A Marching Song

"Yankee Doodle" has been sung in America for more than 200 years! Soldiers in America's Continental Army sang this song as they marched. Now you can **sing** it, too.

★★ Yankee Doodle ★★

Words by Dr. Richard Shuckburgh   *Traditional*

VERSE

1. Fath'r and I went down to camp,

A - long with Cap - tain Good - in'

And there we saw the men and boys

As thick as hast - y pud - din'.

REFRAIN

Yan - kee Doo - dle, keep it up, Yan - kee Doo - dle dan - dy,

Mind the mu - sic and the step And with the girls be hand - y.

2. And there was Captain Washington
   Upon a slappin' stallion,
   A-giving orders to his men;
   I guess there was a million. *Refrain*

Celebrate the Season

CD 1–10
MIDI 27

Reading Sequence 1, page 12

Rhythm: Reading ♩ and ♫

Use rhythm syllables to **read** and **perform** these rhythms with "Go Around the Corn, Sally."

CD 1–17
MIDI 28

Reading Sequence 2, page 14

Rhythm: Reading 𝄽

Use rhythm syllables to **read** and **perform** these rhythms with "*Xiao yin chuan.*"

Melody: Reading *la*

Use pitch syllables to **read** and **sing** this exercise
with "Lucy Locket."

 la

Melody: Reading *so*, *mi*, and *la*

Read and **sing** this exercise with "Pizza, Pizza,
Daddy-o." Use pitch syllables and hand signs.

 so

(Repeat 7 times)

 mi

Music Reading Practice

UNIT 2

Reading Sequence 5, page 44

CD 2–10
MIDI 31

Rhythm: Reading

Read and **perform** these rhythms with "Frog in the Millpond." Use rhythm syllables.

 Reading Sequence 6, page 46

CD 2–15
MIDI 32

Rhythm: Reading

Read and **perform** these rhythms with "Four in a Boat." Use rhythm syllables.

Reading Sequence 7, page 56

CD 2–34
MIDI 33

Melody: Reading *do*

Use pitch syllables to **read** and **sing** this inner-hearing exercise with "Clouds of Gray."

so la so mi so mi do do

so la so mi so mi do do

la

 Reading Sequence 8, page 58

CD 2–39
MIDI 34

so

Melody: Reading *do*

Read and **sing** this melody with "I See the Moon." Use pitch syllables and hand signs.

mi

do

👆 **Reading Sequence 9, page 80**

CD 3–28
MIDI 35

Rhythm: Reading

Use rhythm syllables to **read** and **perform** these rhythms with "Tideo."

👆 **Reading Sequence 10, page 82**

CD 3–35
MIDI 36

Rhythm: Reading

Read and **perform** these rhythms with "Amarillo Armadillo." Use rhythm syllables.

Melody: Reading *re*

Use pitch syllables to **read** and **sing** this inner-hearing exercise with "Rocky Mountain."

la

do   mi   so   la   so   mi   re

do   do   mi   la   so   so   do

so   mi   do   mi   mi   so   re

so   mi   do   mi   so   so   do

so

mi

Reading Sequence 12, page 100

CD 4–14
MIDI 38

Melody: Reading *re*

Read and **sing** this inner-hearing exercise with "Sea Shell." Use pitch syllables and hand signs.

re

do

Reading Sequence 13, page 120

CD 4–41
MIDI 39

Rhythm: Reading ♩, ♫, 𝄾, and ♬♬

Use rhythm syllables to **read** and **perform** this exercise with "Dinah."

Reading Sequence 14, page 125

CD 5–5
MIDI 40

Rhythm: Reading ♩, ♫, ♩‿♩

Read and **perform** these rhythms with *"Frère Jacques."* Use rhythm syllables.

Reading Sequence 15, page 128

CD 5–12
MIDI 41

Melody: Reading *re*

Use pitch syllables to **read** and **sing** this inner-hearing exercise with "How Many Miles to Babylon?"

 Reading Sequence 16, page 135

CD 5–26
MIDI 42

Melody: Reading *do*-Pentatonic

Read and **sing** this melody with *"Ha'kyo jong."* Use pitch syllables and hand signs to practice inner-hearing.

la

so

mi

re

do

Music Reading Practice

Reading Sequence 17, page 158

CD 6–9
MIDI 43

Rhythm: Reading =

Use rhythm syllables to **read** and **perform** these rhythms with *"Hui jia qü."*

Reading Sequence 18, page 160

CD 6–16
MIDI 44

Rhythm: Reading

Read and **perform** these rhythms with *"Un elefante."* Use rhythm syllables.

Melody: Reading a Song That Ends with *do*

Use pitch syllables to **read** and **sing** this exercise
with "All Around the Buttercup."

la

so

 Reading Sequence 20, page 174 CD 6–37
MIDI 46

Melody: Reading a *do*-Pentatonic Song

Read and **sing** this exercise with "*Piñon, pirulín.*"
Use pitch syllables and hand signs.

mi

re

do

Rhythm: Reading Rhythms in 3 Meter

Use rhythm syllables to **read** and **perform** these rhythms with *"Caballito blanco."*

Rhythm: Reading , and

Read and **perform** these rhythms with *"Un, deux, trois."* Use rhythm syllables.

CD 7–44
MIDI 49

Melody: Reading a *do*-Pentatonic Song

Use pitch syllables to **read** and **sing** this exercise with "Great Big House."

la

so

CD 7–51
MIDI 50

Melody: Reading a *do*-Pentatonic Song in G

Read and **sing** this melody with "See-Saw Sacradown." Use pitch syllables and hand signs.

mi

re

do

Mallet Instruments

▲ Soprano xylophone

◀ Alto glockenspiel

Holding the Mallets

It is important to hold the mallets correctly when you play mallet instruments.

▲

Hold the mallets in a relaxed way, almost as if you are riding a bike. Make sure you strike the bar in the center.

Playing Borduns

You can play **borduns** on mallet instruments. Practice the borduns you see here.

> **Borduns** are repeated patterns used to accompany music. They have two pitches, one of which is the home tone.

◀ Alto metallophone

◀ Alto xylophone

419

Sound Bank

◀ **Autoharp** A soundbox with strings across it. When a chord button is pressed, only the strings that fit the chord will sound. **CD 15–16**

◀ **Banjo** A string instrument similar to a guitar but smaller. It has metal strings and a round body. Banjos are often played in a style using fast picking or strumming. **CD 15–17**

◀ **Cello** [CHEH-loh] A large, wooden string instrument. The cello may be plucked with fingers or played with a bow. The cello has a rich, warm voice that can sound quite low. **CD 15–18**

◀ **Clarinet** A wind instrument that has a mouthpiece with a reed. When the player blows into the mouthpiece, the air in the clarinet vibrates, making the sound. **CD 15–19**

◀ **Conga** [KAHN-gah] An Afro-Cuban drum with a long, barrel-shaped body. It comes in three sizes: the small *quinto*, the mid-sized *conga*, and the large *tumbador.* The conga is struck with the fingers and the palms of the hands. **CD 15–20**

◀ **Cymbals** Curved metal plates that come in various sizes. Crash cymbals are played in pairs. The player holds one cymbal in each hand and quickly claps them together. Finger cymbals are tiny and make a delicate ringing sound. **CD 15–21**

◀ **Drum Set** A drum set, or kit, has several drums and cymbals including snare drum, bass drum, tom-toms, and cymbals. **CD 15–22**

◀ **Dulcimer (mountain)** An hourglass-shaped soundbox with three or four strings across it. The strings are usually plucked with a quill. The sound is quiet and sweet. **CD 15–23**

◀ *Dundun* An African instrument with drum heads at each end joined by many strings. As the player strikes one drum head with a beater, the strings are pressed against the side and squeezed by the free arm to change the pitch. In that way the drum can imitate speech. **CD 15–24**

◀ *Erhu* [EHR-hoo] A Chinese string instrument played with a bow. It has only two metal strings. The tube has animal skin covering one end. **CD 15–25**

◀ **Flute** A wind instrument shaped like a metal pipe. The player holds the flute sideways and blows across a mouthpiece. **CD 15–26**

◀ **Guitar** A string instrument from Spain and Latin America, plucked with fingers or a pick. A guitar can play a melody. It can also play chords. Some guitars are electric. They can sound much louder. CD 15–27

◀ **Hammered Dulcimer** A zither-type string instrument, also known as a cymbalom. Metal strings are stretched across bridges and played with spoon-shaped hammers. CD 15–28

◀ **Koto** [KOH-toh] A Japanese string instrument with thirteen long strings. These are set high above the body of the instrument, which sits flat on the floor. The sound is a little like that of a harp. CD 15–29

◀ **Maracas** Large round rattles with handles. They developed in the Caribbean area and in Venezuela. Shaking the maracas makes a crisp "swishing" sound. CD 15–30

◀ **Musical Bow** A string instrument found in Africa. There are many kinds, but the one shown here has a bell attached to make the sound louder. This instrument sounds somewhat like large drops of water. CD 15–31

(422) **Instrument Key:**

Native American Flute A handmade tube-shaped wind instrument, made of wood or clay. The player blows through a hole at one end and finger holes along the body make it possible to change pitches. **CD 15–32**

Pipa [PEE-pah] A Chinese string instrument in the shape of a gourd. It has four strings and is one of the oldest of Chinese instruments. The pipa can play music in a quiet mood as well as in a loud "military style." **CD 15–33**

Shakuhachi [shah-koo-HAH-chee] A Japanese wind instrument made of bamboo. The shakuhachi is a very well-known instrument in Japan. It is played with lots of pitch bends, clicks, and flutters. **CD 15–34**

Sheng [shuhng] A Chinese mouth organ with a bowl-shaped wind chamber made of wood or metal. The sheng has 17 or 19 bamboo pipes of various sizes. The sound of the sheng can be shrill or pleasantly lyrical. **CD 15–35**

String Bass A large wooden string instrument that is either plucked or bowed. The string bass is so tall that a player must stand up or sit on a high stool to play it. The voice of the string bass is deep, dark, and sometimes rumbling. **CD 15–36**

Synthesizer An electronic instrument with a keyboard like a piano. It uses electricity in a special way to make sound. The synthesizer can make many sounds and imitate other instruments. CD 15–37

Tabla [TAH-blah] Hand drums from India. They are usually in sets of two or more. They have a variety of sounds—high, low, loud, pitched, unpitched—that can be produced by striking in different ways and on different parts of the drum head. CD 15–38

Tambourine A round instrument with small metal discs around the edge. Shaking or hitting the tambourine makes a jingling sound. CD 15–39

Timpani Large bowl-shaped drums, also called kettledrums. Unlike many drums, timpani can be tuned to specific pitches. CD 15–40

Trombone A wind instrument made of brass. It makes sound the same way as the trumpet, but the pitches are lower. The player changes pitches by sliding a long curved tube up and down. CD 15–41

Trumpet A wind instrument made of brass. It has a mouthpiece shaped like a little cup. The player makes the sound by "buzzing" the lips into the mouthpiece. The trumpet can sound very loud and military. CD 15–42

◀ **Tuba** A very large brass instrument with a wide bell at one end of coiled tubing. The tuba's low notes are soft and dark-sounding. The higher ones are full and warm. **CD 15–43**

◀ **Viola** [vee-OH-luh] A wooden string instrument that looks like a large violin. The viola is either bowed or plucked. The sound of the viola is deeper, richer, and darker than that of the violin. **CD 15–44**

◀ **Violin** A string instrument that is usually played with a bow. It can also be plucked. The violin plays sounds from low to very high. **CD 15–45**

◀ **Yangqin** [yahng-chin] A Chinese string instrument. It is placed flat on a stand and played with soft mallets. Each string has another underneath. When the string above is played, the one under it vibrates too, making a sweet sustained sound. **CD 14–46**

◀ **Zheng** [chuhng] A Chinese type of plucked zither made of wood. The zheng usually has 16 strings and movable bridges. When playing a zheng, the player uses the fingernails on the right hand to pluck the strings; the left hand is used to apply pressure to the strings. The sound is similar to a harp. **CD 14–47**

Sound Bank

Glossary

AB form A musical plan that has two sections or parts. p. 167

ABA form A musical plan that has three sections or parts. The first and last sections are the same. The middle section is different. p. 201

accent > Gives extra importance to a note in a rhythm pattern. p. 78

accompaniment Music that is performed to go with a melody. p. 142

bar line ≣ A vertical line drawn through a staff to separate measures. p. 83

borduns Repeated patterns used to accompany music. They have two pitches, one of which is the home tone. p. 419

call and response A style of choral singing. First one person sings the call and then the rest of the chorus sings a response, or an answer. p. 19

coda ⊕ A short section added to the end of a song. p. 168

crescendo ⎯⎯ A word or music symbol that tells the performer to get gradually louder. p. 116

cumulative song A song that gets longer as each new verse is added. p. 360

D.C. al Fine An Italian phrase that tells the performer to go back to the beginning of the song and sing until the word *Fine*. p. 200

dynamics A word that describes the loudness or softness of music. p. 6

fermata ⌒ A symbol that tells a performer to hold a note for an extra long time. p. 191

form The order of same and different ideas in music. p. 52

forte *f* loud. p. 6

improvise To make up music as it is being performed. p. 219

introduction A short section placed at the beginning of a song. p. 345

ledger line ♩ An extra line used for pitches above or below the staff. p. 101

legato Describes a melody that has smooth, connected pitches p. 152

measure ≣ A grouping of beats separated by bar lines. p. 83

melody A row of pitches that move up or down or repeat. p. 24

meter The way beats of music are grouped together. They are often in sets of two or sets of three. p. 196

note A symbol for a musical sound. p. 78

ostinato A short repeated pattern. p. 35

pentatonic Songs that have only five pitches. p. 136

percussion Instruments that are played by shaking, scraping, or striking. p. 102

phrase A musical sentence. p. 126

piano *p* soft. p. 6

pitch Another word for a musical note. Pitch is how high or how low a note sounds. p. 21

pitch syllables Syllables used to name pitches, for example: *do, re, mi, so,* and *la.* p. 27

refrain The section of a song that repeats, using the same melody and words. p. 191

repeated pitches Two or more pitches in a row that are the same. p. 61

rhythm A pattern of long and short sounds and silences. p. 10

rhythm syllables Syllables used to name specific rhythmic units. p. 17

section A part of a song or instrumental work. p. 166

skip Moving from one pitch to another, skipping one or more pitches in between. p. 61

staccato Describes a melody that has short, separated pitches. p. 152

staff A set of five horizontal lines on which music notes are written. p. 27

steady beat The regular pulse found in most music. p. 8

step Moving from one pitch to another with no skipped pitches in between. p. 61

strong beat The most important beat in a rhythm pattern. p. 50

style The special sound that is created when music elements, such as rhythm and timbre, are combined. p. 254

technique The special skill used to play an instrument. p. 65

tempo The speed of the beat in music. p. 42

texture How thin or thick the music sounds. p. 71

tie A musical symbol that joins two notes together to create a longer sound. p. 125

timbre The special sound each instrument makes. p. 64

Classified Index

Listening selections appear in *italics*

Folk, Traditional, and Regional Selections

African American
Bob-a-Needle 232
Chicka Hanka 211
Down, Down, Baby 32
Free at Last 396
Go Around the Corn, Sally 12
Good Mornin', Blues 52
I Got Shoes 242
Kid Like Me, A (speech piece) 394
Kwanzaa Carol, A 392
Michael, Row the Boat Ashore 18
Miss Mary Mack 42
Rosie, Darling Rosie 215
Same Train 164
Sleep, Baby, Sleep (Creole) 197
This Little Light of Mine 241
Way Down in the Schoolyard 50
Way Down Yonder in the Brickyard 51
When a Man's a Long Way from Home 53
When the Saints Go Marching In 179
When the Saints Go Marching In 178

American Indian. *See* Native American.

Brazil
Chica chica boom chic 112
Ciranda (A Ring of Roses) 272
Concerto for Marimba and String Orchestra, "Saudação" 119
Kibungo 354
O pião entrou (The Top Joined the Circle) 355

Central America
Piñon, pirulín, 174

Chile
Un elefante (An Elephant) 160

China
Diou shou juan'er (Hide the Scarf) 277
Hui jia qü (Home from School) 158

Xiao yin chuan (Silver Moon Boat) 14

Costa Rica
Mariposita (Little Butterfly) 156

Denmark
Der sad to katte (Two Cats) 300

Ecuador
El juego chirimbolo (The "Chirimbolo" Game) 54

England. *See also* United Kingdom.
Cold and Frosty Morning 139
How Many Miles to Babylon? 128
Tree in the Wood, The 360

France
Frère Jacques (Are You Sleeping?) 125
Mon papa (My Papa) 280
Un, deux, trois (One, Two, Three) 198

Germany
Ein Männlein steht im Walde (A Little Man in the Woods) 90
Hänsel und Gretel, "Ein Männlein steht im Walde" 91
O laufet, ihr Hirten (Come Running, You Shepherds) 384

Ghana
Ayelivi 70
Che che koolay 266

Haiti
Deau-deau, ti pitit maman (Sleep, My Little One) 306

Indonesia
Ujan mas (Golden Rain) (Bali) 105

Israeli/Jewish/Hebrew
Achshav (Awake! Awake!) 64
Chanukah Is Here! 382
Ner li (The Light) 383
Perot (Fruit) 378

Japan
Haru ga kita (Springtime Has Come) 401
Tanabata-sama (Star Festival) 336

Korea
Arirang 137
Ha'kyo jong (School Bell Sounding) 135

Latin America
Naranja dulce (Sweet Orange) (Mexico and Costa Rica) 96

Mexico
Allá en la fuente (There at the Spring) 92
Caballito blanco (Little White Pony) 193
El tambor (The Drum) 274

Native American
Chuhwuht (Pima) 356
Duck Dance (Seminole and Choctaw) 249
Rain Song, The (Navajo) 323
Song of the Eagle (Wechihit-Yokuts) 248
Tall Cedar Tree (Lummi) 322

New Zealand
Haere (Farewell) 285

Nicaragua
Banana 114

Nigeria
Ise oluwa 102

Puerto Rico
Cheki, morena (Shake It!) 180
El coquí (The Little Frog) 292
El florón (The Flower) 246

South Africa
Abiyoyo 108

Spain
La mar estaba serena (The Sea is Calm) 345
Un pajarito (A Little Bird) 16

Switzerland
L'inverno è passato (Winter Is Over) 400

Tanzania
Kou ri lengay (The Strength of the Lion) 217

Thailand
Sawatdee tuh jah (The Hello Song) 265

Trinidad and Tobago
Boysie 195

Turkey
Adana ya gidelim (Let's Go to Adana) 142

United Kingdom. *See also* England.
Leatherwing Bat 303

United States. *See also* African American, Native American, Puerto Rico.
A-Tisket, A-Tasket 238
A-Tisket, A-Tasket 239
All Around the Buttercup 170
Banjo Sam (North Carolina) 314
Boogie Chant and Dance (speech piece) 78
Crocodile, The 362
Deux cocodries (Two Crocodiles) (Louisiana Cajun) 364
Dinah 120
Down the Ohio 60
Farmer's Dairy Key, The 182
Four in a Boat (Appalachia) 46
Frog in the Millpond 44
Great Big House (Louisiana) 204
I Bought Me a Cat (Kentucky) 308
I Fed My Horse (North Carolina) 94
I See the Moon 58
Jelly in a Dish (speech piece) 83
Kapulu kane (Puili Game Song) (Hawaii) 270
L'arc en ciel (The Arch in the Sky) (Louisiana Cajun) 333
Lone Star Trail 21
Lucy Locket 27
My Father's House (Southern U.S.) 25
My Foot's In My Stirrup (Tennessee) 234
Oh, Watch the Stars (South Carolina) 144
Old Brass Wagon 122
Patty Cake Polka 281
Pizza, Pizza, Daddy-o 28
Rainbow, The 332
Rocky Mountain (Southern U.S.) 98

Shake Them 'Simmons Down (Texas) 244
She'll Be Comin' 'Round the Mountain
   (Southern U.S.) 358
Shenandoah 62
Shoo, Fly 200
Skin and Bones (Kentucky) 376
Somebody Waiting 283
Tideo (Texas) 80
Two Little Sausages (speech piece) 79
We're All Gonna Shine Tonight 240
Zudio 269

Venezuela
El tren (The Train) 260

West Africa
Primitive Fire, "Oya" 69

West Indies
Cookie 172

Zimbabwe
Chawe chidyo chem'chero 297

Holiday, Seasonal, and Special Occasion

Chanukah
Chanukah Is Here! 382
Ner li (The Light) 383

Christmas
Christmas, Don't Be Late 386
It's Santa—Again! 385
O laufet, ihr Hirten (Come Running, You
   Shepherds) 384

General
It's a Celebration! 372
Vamos a la fiesta (Let's Go to the Party) 374

Halloween
Owl and the Pumpkin, The 377
Skin and Bones 376

Kwanzaa
Kwanzaa Carol, A 392

Martin Luther King, Jr. Day
Free at Last 396
Kid Like Me, A 394

Patriotic
America 403
America, I Hear You Singing 402
Yankee Doodle 405

Spring
Haru ga kita (Springtime Has Come) 401
L'inverno è passato (Winter Is Over) 400

Sukkot
Perot (Fruit) 378

Thanksgiving
Thanksgiving Is Near 380

Valentine's Day
Valentines 398

Winter
Frosty, the Snowman 391
Jingle Bells 388
Mister Snow Rap 391
Sleigh Ride 390

Listening Selections

Anderson: *Sleigh Ride* 390 **CD 14–32**
Arbeau: *Pavane et Gaillarde* 279 **CD 10–16**
Bartók: *For Children (Sz 42), Volume II,*
   "Allegro non troppo, No. 33" 49
   CD 2–20
Beach: *Les Rêves de Columbine, Op. 65,*
   "Sous les étoiles" 338 **CD 12–16**
Burch: *Rain Song, The* 323 **CD 11–32**
Carleton: *Ja-Da* 187 **CD 7–12**
Carpenter: *Halley Came to Jackson* 341
   CD 12–18
Copland: *Rodeo*, "Buckaroo Holiday"
   (excerpt) 23 **CD 1–28**
Creamer/Layton: *After You've Gone* 189
   CD 7–15
Diallo: Nangapè 103 **CD 4–20**
Doucet: *L'arc en ciel* 333 **CD 12–8**

Gaye, Stevenson, and Hunter: *Dancing in the Street* 254 CD 9–17

Grainger: *Free Music #1* 212 CD 8–3

Handel: *Solomon,* "Arrival of the Queen of Sheba, The" 348 CD 12–27

Hanson: *Toccata and Tango* 154 CD 5–52

Haydn: *Symphony in G, No. 88,* "Movement 4" 84 CD 3–40

Humperdinck: *Hänsel und Gretel,* "Ein Männlein steht im Walde" 91 CD 3–47

Joplin: *Entertainer, The* 76 CD 3–21

Keetman: *Allegretto* 131 CD 5–19

Knaack: *3 + 2* 316 CD 11–25

Ledbetter: *When a Man's a Long Way from Home* 53 CD 2–26

Louiselle: *Disco Worm* 312 CD 11–21

Mancini: *Baby Elephant Walk* 163 CD 6–19

McCutcheon and Kahn: *Stick Together* 231 CD 8–18

Moross: *Big Country, The* 236 CD 8–23

Morton: *Kansas City Stomp* 251 CD 9–14

Olatunji: *Primitive Fire,* "Oya" 69 CD 3–8

Prokofiev: *Symphony No. 1 in D Major,* "Gavotte" 338 CD 12–17

Puente: *Loco bossa nova* 247 CD 9–5

Puente: *Oye como va* 255 CD 9–18

Puente: *Vaya Puente* 181 CD 7–5

Red Hot Chili Peppers: *Yertle the Turtle* 368 CD 13–27

Respighi: *Fontane di Roma* (Fountains of Rome), "La fontana di Trevi al meriggio" 93 CD 3–52

Rodrigo: *Concierto Madrigal for Two Guitars and Orchestra,* "Fanfarre" 150 CD 5–49

Rollins and Nelson: *Frosty, the Snowman* 391 CD 14–33

Rosauro: *Concerto for Marimba and String Orchestra,* "Saudação" 119 CD 4–38

Stravinsky: *Greeting Prelude* 264 CD 9–27

Traditional African American: *This Little Light of Mine* 241 CD 8–29

Traditional African American: *Way Down Yonder in the Brickyard* 51 CD 2–23

Traditional African American: *When the Saints Go Marching In* 179 CD 6–43

Traditional American: *Liberty/Chicken Reel* 38 CD 2–1

Traditional American: *A-Tisket, A-Tasket* 239 CD 8–26

Traditional American: *Patty Cake Polka* 281 CD 10–21

Traditional American: *Rumblin On* 315 CD 11–24

Traditional American River Shanty: *Shenandoah* 62 CD 2–46

Traditional Balinese: *Ujan mas* (Golden Rain) 105 CD 4–22

Traditional English: *Cold and Frosty Morning* 139 CD 5–30

Traditional Korean: *Arirang* 137 CD 5–29

Traditional Mexican: *El tilingo lingo* 176 CD 6–40

Waldteufel: *Les Patineurs* (The Skaters) 387 CD 14–29

Warren and Gordon: *Chica chica boom chic* 112 CD 4–31

Whelan: *Riverdance Suite* 141 CD 5–31

Williams: *Sinfonia Antarctica,* "Epilogue" 326 CD 11–35

Poems and Stories

Around the World 256

Breaks Free 319

Chawe chidyo chem'chero 296 CD 11–1

De Beat 67 CD 3–7

Flies 201

How Doth the Little Crocodile 363

Kibungo, Beast of the Forest 352 CD 13–1

Rabbits 305

Setting the Thanksgiving Table 381

Stars Streaming in the Sky, The 357

To a Red Kite 326

Way Down in the Music 227

When I Grow Up 397

Wind Has Shaken Autumn Down 57

Recorded Interviews

Liam Burke 11 CD 1–7

Igor Stravinsky 264 CD 9–27

Credits

Design Electronic Production: Kirchoff/Wohlberg, Inc.

Listening Maps and Music Reading Practice: MediaLynx Design Group

Photograph Credits

2 © Bert Essel/The Stock Market 2 © Jim Erckson/The Stock Market 3 © Mark Richards/PhotoEdit 6 Robert Brenner/PhotoEdit 6 © Dean Berry/Liaison Agency 6 Tony Freeman/PhotoEdit 10 ©Joan Marcus 11 ©Joan Marcus 28 Artville 43 ©The Estate of Keith Haring 47 Terry Vine/Stone 48 Collections Mnam/Cci-Centre Georges Pompidou/"Photo: Phototheque des collections du Mnam/Cci"/Art Resource, NY 53 Bernard Hoffman/LIFE Magazine©Time Inc. 55 Ric Ergenbight/Ric Ergenbright 65 Terry Vine/Stone 66 Warren Johnson/Marilyn Rife 66 Jack Vartoogian 67 Photograph by Michael Dames/Soh Daiko, New York 67 Rudi Von Briel/PhotoEdit 67 ©Neil Zlozower/Neil Zlozower Photography 68 H & E Bernheim/Woodfin Camp & Associates 68 © Errington/The Hutchison Library 68 The Newark Museum/Art Resource, NY 68 PhotoDisc 69 Jack Vartoogian 69 © Mary Jelliffe/The Hutchison Library 75 Walt Disney/Kobal Collection 77 Nina Mera 79 ©Estate of Roy Lichtenstein 82 PhotoDisc 84 Courtesy of WTTW, Chicago IL 84 © Gianni Dagli Orti/Corbis 86 Philip Gould/Corbis 88 Philip Gould/Corbis 89 Robert Fried Photography 91 Photo © Jack Vartoogian 92 ©Glen Allison/Stone 93 Greg Probst/Stock Boston 93 Black Star 93 ©Stephen Studd/Stone 99 Corbis 100 (Bkgd) William J. Hebert/Getty Images 102 Tibor Bognar/Stock Market 102 ©Mark Lewis/Stone 103 Werner Forman/Art Resource, NY 104 Getty Images 105 Dr. Kuo-Huang Han 106 Getty Images 107 Getty Images 109 Pete Seeger's Storysong "Abiyoyo"/Illustrated by Michael Hays 110 Brand X Pictures 112 Brand X Pictures 113 Everett Collection, Inc. 114 Dave King/© Dorling Kindersley 114 Flag Research Center 115 © Dorling Kindersley 116 Jon G. Fuller/Natural Selection Stock Photography, Inc. 117 Jon G. Fuller/Natural Selection Stock Photography, Inc. 121 Gift of Mrs. Jane C. Carey as an addition to the Addie Burr Clark Memorial Collection, ©2000 Board of Trustees, National Gallery of Art, Washington, D.C. 139 Michael Le Poer Trench/Riverdance The Show 142 Sitki Tarlan/Panoramic Images 142 Scala/Art Resource, NY 154 Pearl Corporation and Adams 158 PhotoDisc 166 (Bkgd) Michael Giannechini/Photo Researchers, Inc. 170 (Bkgd) © Martin Barraud/the Image Bank/Getty Images 170 (TL) ©Dorling Kindersley 179 AP/Wide World 183 Michael Boys/Corbis 189 (BR) ©Hulton Archive/Getty Images 202 ©Charles Webb/AppaLight 203 Private Collection Kathleen Cunningham 212 Getty Images 212 Big Briar 216 Corbis 218 © Staffan Widstrand/Corbis 224 John Running/@2000 John Running 224 Teri Bloom Photography, Inc 224 © Kevin Fleming/Corbis 225 Daniel J. Gandor 225 © Joseph Sohm; ChromoSohm Inc./Corbis 225 Photofest 226 © Joe Viesti/Viesti Collection, Inc. 226 SuperStock 227 © Steve Kaufman/Corbis 227 © Jay Syverson/Corbis 227 © Kevin R. Morris/Corbis 238 Getty Images 240 Getty Images 241 ©Arthur Tilley/Getty Images/FPG 241 SuperStock 248 Lynn Wozniak/All One Tribe, Inc. 249 Peter B. Gallagher, Seminole Communications 252 (TR) Corbis 253 (BC) ©Hulton Archive/Getty Images 255 Reed Saxon/AP/Wide World 264 Musee d'Orsay, Paris/Photograph by Erich Lessing/Art Resource, NY 264 Cary Wolinsky/Stock Boston 264 SuperStock 265 Bill Bachmann/PhotoEdit 266 David Young-Wolff/PhotoEdit 267 ©Victor Englebert 273 ©1988/Brenda Joysmith Studio 274 (TR) © Ron Watts/Corbis 278 Photograph by Erich Lessing/Art Resource, NY 286 © H. Joseph Sohm 287 © Bob Torrez/Stone 287 © Robert Eckert/Stock Boston 287 Robert Amft 291 Banana Slug String Band 294 © Mark Gamba/The Stock Market 294 PhotoDisc 296 (BC) Frank Greenaway/©Dorling Kindersley 296 (Bkgd) Ian Murphy/Getty Images 298 (Bkgd) Harvey Lloyd/Getty Images 302 © Stephen Dalton/Photo Researchers, Inc. 306 © Algaze/Image Works 307 Galerie Macondo 307 Pictor 314 (Bkgd) © David Muench/Getty Images/Stone 315 (BL) Henry Ossawa Tanner, The Banjo Lesson, 1893. Oil on canvas. Hampton University Museum, Hampton, Virginia/Hampton University Museum 322 Northwest Indian College 323 @2000 John Running 334 Schalkwijk/Art Resource, NY 334 SuperStock 338 Corbis 340 © 1999 by Dan Andreasen/Courtesy, HarperCollins Publishers 343 © Henry Diltz/Corbis 344 (Bkgd) © Michelle Chaplow/Corbis 346 Getty Images 347 Getty Images 348 (Bkgd) Barry Winiker/Index Stock Imagery 348 (BL) © Archivo Iconografico,S.A./Corbis 372 © David Young-Wolff/PhotoEdit 372 © Barbara Stitzer/PhotoEdit 372 Getty Images 373 © Lawrence Migdale/www.migdale.com 373 Getty Images 374 Haga Library Inc. 380 Brand X Pictures 380 Getty Images 382 © Bill Aron/Photo Researchers, Inc. 387 (TR) Gilbert Stuart, The Skater (Portrait of William Grant), Andrew Mellon collection, Image © 2003 Board of Trustees, National Gallery of Art, Washington/National Gallery of Art 389 Holiday Sleigh Ride by Jane Wooster Scott/© 1994 JWS Inc./Jane Wooster Scott Photo by John Tweedle 395 AP/Wide World 400 © William Manning/The Stock Market 402 Joe Sohm/© Visions of America, LLC 2000 405 The Continentals by Frank Blackwell Mayer, Smithsonian American Art Museum, Washington, DC/Art Resource, NY

Illustrations

2 Bert VanderMark 6 Rose Mary Berlin 8 Mary Ross 12 Georgia Cawley 13 Georgia Cawley 14 Dom Lee 20 Joel Spector 21 Joel Spector 22 Joel Spector 23 Joel Spector 24 Linda Graves 26 Franklin Hammond 32 Georgia Cawley 34 Jack Davis 38 Bert VanderMark 46 Terry Taylor 46 Kelly Hume 50 Guy Porfirio 51 Guy Porfirio 55 Annette Cable 56 David Diaz Courtesy David Diaz 58 Anthony Lewis 60 Jennifer Thermes 62 Jennifer Thermes 63 Jennifer Thermes 68 Kelly Hume 71 Donna Perrone 73 Donna Perrone 76 Michael Sternagle 78 Georgia Cawley 80 Susan Spellman 81 Susan Spellman 82 Laura De Santis 83 Laura De Santis 86 Tim Huhn 91 Lorraine Ryan 94 Liz Callen 96 Liz Callen 100 David Diaz 101 David Diaz 106 George Hamblin 116 Kelly Hume 120 Kelly Hume 120 Byron Gin 123 Sam Whitaker 123 Alexi Natchev 124 Alexi Natchev 128 Fahimeh Amiri 130 Rusty Fletcher 131 Rusty Fletcher 132 Tim Spransy 132 Kelly Hume 134 Chi Chung 136 Chi Chung 138 Francesco Santalucia 138 Kelly Hume 140 Tony Nuccio 144 Wendy Rasmussen 144 Kelly Hume 149 Gwen Connelly 152 Lyn Martin 153 Lyn Martin 154 Lyn Martin 157 Marcela Cabrera 158 Chi Chung 159 Chi Chung 161 Kathi Ember 162 Kathi Ember 163 Kathi Ember 164 Milan Kecman 165 Susan Swan 168 Susan Swan 169 Susan Swan 172 Higgins Bond 176 Claudia Hammer 177 Claudia Hammer 178 Marc Mongeau 182 Kelly Hume 186 Mark Riedy 188 Mark Riedy 190 Diane Greenseid 191 Diane Greenseid 192 Eileen Mueller Neill 193 Eileen Mueller Neill 194 Tom Leonard 194 Christopher Corr 195 Christopher Corr 195 Christopher Corr 200 Jared Lee 201 Jared Lee 204 Milan Kecman 205 Milan Kecman 207 Julie Peterson 208 Julie Peterson 210 Tom Foty 213 Tony Nuccio 221 Milan Kecman 228 Elizabeth Sayles 230 Elizabeth Sayles 234 Jerry Tiritilli 235 Jerry Tiritilli 236 Jerry Tiritilli 237 Jerry Tiritilli 238 Beth Foster Wiggins 238 Kelly Hume 238 Beth Foster Wiggins 239 Joel Spector 240 Kelly Hume 242 Higgins Bond 244 Susan Swan 246 Joel Spector 248 Dorothy Sullivan 249 Dorothy Sullivan 250 John Hovell 252 George Baquero 256 Ilene Robinette 258 Ilene Robinette 260 David McCall Johnston 266 268 Priscilla Burris 269 Priscilla Burris 272 Jill Banashek 276 Cheryl Kirk Noll 278 Wayne McLoughlin 279 Tony Nuccio 280 Wayne McLoughlin 281 Wayne McLoughlin 282 Cornelius Van Wright 284 Dorothy Sullivan 284 Kelly Hume 285 Kelly Hume 288 Gary Torrisi 289 Gary Torrisi 290 Gary Torrisi 292 Kristin Kest 300 Donna Catanese 302 Jerry Tiritilli 304 Eileen Mueller Neill 308 Paul Larson 310 Larry Reinhart 312 Larry Reinhart 313 Larry Reinhart 316 Jill Banashek 318 Jill Banashek 319 Jill Banashek 320 Jane Dippold 322 Wayne Parmenter 324

Shelly Shinjo 326 Shelly Shinjo 328 Sam Whitaker 330 Tim Huhn 336 Oki Han 338 Oki Han 342 Kelly Hume 342 Higgins Bond 350 Toby Williams 352 Peter Fasolino 353 Peter Fasolino 354 Peter Fasolino 356 Shelly Hehenberger 360 Georgia Cawley 362 Dan McGeehan 364 Teri Sloat 364 Kelly Hume 366 John Sandford 368 Dan McGeehan 370 Dan McGeehan 373 Tony Nuccio 376 C. D. Hullinger 377 C. D. Hullinger 378 David Austin Clar 378 David Austin Clar 378 Kelly Hume 380 Gregg Thorkelson 382 Leslie Watkins 383 Leslie Watkins 384 Karen Pritchett 385 Karen Pritchett 386 Gwen Connelly 388 Jeremy Tugeau 390 Jeremy Tugeau 397 Higgins Bond 398 Nancy Tobin

Acknowledgments

Credits and appreciation are due publishers and copyright owners for use of the following:
4: "Gonna Have a Good Time" Words and Music by Bill Shontz, from *Rosenshontz: Share It!* 1992 Rosho Music. Reprinted by Permission. 6: "Heigh-Ho" Words by Larry Morey, music by Frank Churchill. © Copyright 1938 by Bourne Co. Copyright Renewed. This arrangement © 2002 by Bourne Co. All Rights Reserved. International Copyright Secured. Reprinted by permission. 8: "Time to Sing" Music by Raffi, Words by Raffi, D. Pike, B & B Simpson. ©1985 Homeland Publishing (CAPAC). A division of Troubadour Records Ltd. All rights reserved. Used by permission. 16: "Un pajarito" (A Little Bird) ["El pajaro" (The Bird)], from *A Fiesta of Folk Songs from Spain & Latin America* by Henrietta Yurchenco, copyright ©1967 by Henrietta Yurchenco. Used by permission of G.P. Putnam's Sons, a divison of Penguin Putnam Inc. English version by Pearson Education, Inc. 28: "Pizza, Pizza, Daddy-o" from *Circle 'Round the Zero* by Maureen Kenney and MMB Music, Inc. 1974. Reprinted by Permission. 40: "The Music's in Me" Words and Music by Jill Gallina. Copyright ©1985 by Jenson Publications. This arrangement copyright ©2001 by Jenson Publications. International Copyright Secured. All Rights Reserved. Used by Permission. 44: "Frog in the Millpond" (Frog in the Meadow) Additional words ©2002 Pearson Education, Inc. 50: "Way Down in the Schoolyard" from *In the Schoolyard* by Sharon Lois & Bram. Used by permission of Elephant Records. 52: "Good Mornin', Blues" New words and new music arranged by Huddie Ledbetter. Edited and new additional material by Alan Lomax. TRO—© Copyright 1959 (Renewed) Folkways Music Publishers, Inc., New York, NY. Used by Permission. 54: "El juego chirimbolo" (The Chirimbolo Game) from *Roots and Branches: A Legacy of Multicultural Music for Children* by Patricia Shehan Campbell, Ellen McCullough-Brabson, and Judith Cook Tucker. Courtesy World Music Press. Used by permission of World Music Press. English version by Pearson Education, Inc. 56: "Clouds of Gray" from *Kodaly in Kindergarten*, (BK-15) Words and Music by Katinka S. Daniel, Copyright ©1981 Mark Foster Music Co., a division of Shawnee Press, Inc. Delaware Water Gap, PA 18327. International Copyright Secured. All Rights Reserved. Reprinted by Permission. 57: "Wind Has Shaken Autumn Down" by Tony Johnston. Copyright ©1990 by Tony Johnston. Reprinted by arrangement with the author and Writers House LLC, acting as agent for the author. 67: "De Beat" by Grace Nichols. Reproduced with permission of Curtis Brown Ltd, London, on behalf of Grace Nichols. Copyright Grace Nichols 1989. Reprinted by Permission. 70: "Ayelivi" arranged by Komla Amoaku from *The Ewe speaking people of Ghana*. Reprinted by Permission. English version by Pearson Education, Inc. 74: "Step in Time" Words and Music by Richard M. Sherman and Robert B. Sherman. ©1963 Wonderland Music Company, Inc. All Rights Reserved. Reprinted by Permission. 78: "Boogie Chant and Dance" from *Rhythm Road: Poems to Dance To*. Words by Lillian Morrison. Copyright ©1988 by Lillian Morrison. Used by permission of HarperCollins Publishers. 79: "Two Little Sausages" from *Anna Banana: 101 Jump-Rope Rhymes* by Joanna Cole. Text copyright ©1989 by Joanna Cole. Used by permission of HarperCollins Publishers. Rhythmic setting © 2002 Pearson Education, Inc. 82: "Amarillo Armadillo" Words and Music by Robert Demmert. Copyright ©2002 Red Room Studios. 83: "Jelly in a Dish" from *Anna Banana: 101 Jump-Rope Rhymes*. Words by Joanna Cole. Text copyright ©1989 By Joanna Cole. Used by permission of HarperCollins Publishers. Rhythmic setting ©2002 Pearson Education, Inc. 86: "Crawfish!" Words and Music by Papillion ©1997, Papillion Inc. publisher, from the album *Cajun for Kids!* Papillion, Music for Little People/Label. Reprinted by Permission. 90: "Ein Männlein steht im Walde" (A Little Man in the Woods), poem by Hoffmann von Fallersleben. Traditional music. Publication: Sing Mit, Unterstufe. Printed by R. Oldenbourg Verlag, München 1975. Used with permission. English version by Pearson Education, Inc. 92: "Alla en la fuente" (There in the Fountain) from *Arroz Con* edited and illustrated by Lulu Delacre. Copyright ©1989 by Lulu Delacre. Reprinted by Permission of Scholastic Inc. English version by Pearson Education, Inc. 94: "I Fed My Horse" from *The Kodaly Context* by Lois Choksy. © 1981 by Prentice-Hall, Inc. Reprinted by permission of Pearson Education, Inc., Upper Saddle River, NJ. 95: "Naranja dulce" (Sweet Orange) English words ©2002 Pearson Education, Inc. 98: "Rocky Mountain" folk song from Southern United States. ©1972 (Renewed) Belwin, Inc. All Rights Reserved. Used by Permission. WARNER BROS. PUBLICATIONS U.S. INC., Miami, FL 33014. 100: "Sea Shell" Words and Music by Pierre Perron. Reprinted by permission of Pierre Perron. 102: "Ise Oluwa" a Yoruba Song from Nigeria, arranged by Nitanju Bolande Casel. Copyright ©1989 by Nitanju Bolande Casel, Clear Ice Music. Used by permission. 107: "Waiting for the Traffic Light" ©2002 Pearson Education, Inc. 114: "Banana" from *Rainbow Sign*. Words and Music by Flor de Caña. Reprinted by Permission. 116: "La tormenta tropical" (The Tropical Storm) ©2000 Juanita Newland-Ulloa, ASCAP. 126: "A Song That's Just for You" Words and Music by Bryan Louiselle. ©2000 Bryan Louiselle and Frog Prince Music. 130: "Plant Four Seeds" from *Music For Children Volume 1*. American Version by Carl Orff and Gunild Keetman. ©1982 Schott Music Corp. All Rights Reserved. Used by permission of European American Music Distributors LLC, Sole U.S. and Canadian Agent for Schott Music Corp. 132: "Mississippi River Chant" from *Sounds of a Powwow*. Words by Bill Martin, Jr. Used with the permission of the author. 135: "Ha'kyo jong" (School Bell Sounding) Words and Music by Mary Kimm Joh from *Roots & Branches: A Legacy of Multicultural Music for Children* by Patricia Shehan Campbell, Ellen McCullough-Brabson, and Judith Cook Tucker. Courtesy World Music Press. English version by Pearson Education, Inc. 142: "Adana ya gidelim" (Let's Go to Adana) English words ©2002 Pearson Education, Inc. 144: "Oh, Watch the Stars" from *Folk Songs North America Sings* by Richard Johnston. 1984 by Caveat Music Publishing Ltd., copyright assigned 1988 to G. Ricordi & Co. (Canada) Ltd. Used with Permission. 148: "I See With My Hands" Words and Music by Marcy Marxer, from *Cathy and Marcy: Nobody Else Like Me*. ©1993, 2 Spoons Music (ASCAP). Used with Permission. 152: "Party Tonight!" Words and Music by Jill Gallina ©2000 Jill Gallina. 156: "Mariposita" (Little Butterfly) English words ©2002 Pearson Education, Inc. 158: "Hui jia qü" (Home from School) Melody copyright ©1946 the Pagoda, World Around Songs, Inc. English version by Silver Burdett Ginn. 160: "Un elefante" Words and Music by Claudina de Ferrari, from *Musica Folklorica y Popular Infantil Chilena* by Juan Pérez Ortega. Reprinted by Permission. English verson by Pearson Education, Inc. 164: "Same Train" from *Sing a Song* by Charity Bailey ©1955 (renewed) Plymouth Music Co., Inc. Reprinted by Permission. 166: "Sing A Rainbow," Words and Music by Arthur Hamilton. © 1955 (Renewed) Mark VII Ltd. All rights administered by WB Music Corp. All Rights Reserved. Used by Permission. WARNER BROS. PUBLICATIONS U.S. INC., Miami, FL. 33014. 168: "Dinosaur Dance" Words and Music by Ned Ginsburg. ©1991 by Ned Ginsburg. Reprinted by Permission. 170: "All Around the Buttercup" from *Let's Sing Together* by Denise Bacon. ©Copyright 1971 by Boosey & Hawkes, Inc. Copyright renewed. Reprinted by Permission of Boosey & Hawkes, Inc. 172: "Cookie" from *Leading Young Children to Music*, 6E by Haines and Gerber, ©2000. Reprinted by permission of Prentice-Hall, Inc., Upper Saddle River, NJ. 174: "Piñon, pirulín" from *Fiesta! Mexico and*

Central America: A Global Awareness Program for Children, Grades 2-5. Reprinted with permission from ©1993 by Children's Publishing a division of School Specialty, Inc. English version by Pearson Education, Inc. 180: "Cheki Morena" (Shake It !) as remembered by Richardo Morla Rios in *Roots and Branches: A Legacy of Multicultural Music for Children*, by Patricia Shehan Campbell, Ellen McCullough-Brabson, and Judith Cook Tucker. Used by permission. English version by Pearson Education, Inc. 188: "Ja-Da," Words and Music by Bob Carleton, with Revised lyrics by Nan Lynn & Ken Lane. 1918, 1939 (Copyrights Renewed) EMI Feist Catalog Inc. All Rights Reserved. Used by Permission. WARNER BROS. PUBLICATIONS U.S. INC., Miami, FL. 33014. 190: "But the Cat Came Back" Words and Music by Josef Marais. (ASCAP) ©1956, 1984. Used by permission of Marcel Demiranda. 195: "Boysie" from *The Melody Book* by Patricia Hackett. ©1983. Reprinted by permission of Prentice-Hall, Inc., Upper Saddle River, NJ. 197: "Sleep, Baby, Sleep" from *Shake It To The One That You Love Best* adapted by Cheryl Warren Mattox. Reprinted with permission. 201: "Flies" from *All Together* by Dorothy Aldis, copyright 1925-1928, 1934, 1939, 1952, renewed 1953, ©1954-1956, 1962 by Dorothy Aldis, ©1967 by Roy E. Porter, renewed. Used by permission of G.P. Putnam's Sons, a divison of Penguin Putnam Inc. 202: "Trouble Is a Mountain" Words and Music by Arthur Cunningham. Copyright ©1979. Used by permission of Mrs. Arthur Cunningham. 208: "See-Saw Sacradown" Music by Paul Kapp from *A Cat Came Fiddling and Other Rhymes of Childhood*, published by Harcourt Brace, 1956. Reprinted by permission by Richard Kapp. 212: "Free Music No. 1" tracing of a score by Percy Grainger. Reproduced by kind permission of Bardic Edition. 215: "Rosie, Darling Rosie." ©Copyright 1974 by Boosey & Hawkes, Inc. Reprinted by permission of Boosey & Hawkes, Inc. 217: "Kou ri lengay" (The Strength of the Lion) by Beatrice Landeck, from *Echoes of Africa* in Folk Songs of the Americas. Used by permission of Olga Rothchild and Edith Langner. 226: "Ev'ry Kind of Music" Words and Music by David Eddleman. ©1991 David Eddleman. Used by permission. All Rights Reserved. 227: "Way Down in the Music" by Eloise Greenfield from *Honey I Love*. Text copyright ©1978 by Eloise Greenfield. Reprinted by permission of HarperCollins Publishers. 228: "Glad to Have a Friend Like You" from *Free to Be...You and Me*. Words and Music by Carol Hall. ©Copyright 1999 Otay Music, Corp. and Daniel Music (ASCAP). Reprinted by Permission. 232: "Bob-a-Needle" ©2002 Pearson Education, Inc. 234: "My Foot's in My Stirrup" from *Sing It Yourself*. Copyright 1978 by Alfred Publishing Co., Inc. All Rights Reserved. Used with Expressed Written Permission of Publisher. 240: "We're All Gonna Shine Tonight" Words and Music by Marie Winn and Allan Miller from *The Fireside Book of Fun and Games*, published by Simon & Schuster. Music and lyrics copyright © 1966, renewed 1994 by Marie Winn and Allan Miller. Reprinted by Permission. 242: "I Got Shoes" ©2002 Pearson Education, Inc. 246: "El florón" (The Flower) English words ©1988 Silver Burdett Ginn. 249: "Duck Dance" ©1998 Seventh Generation Music. 252: "Happy Feet," Words by Jack Yellen and Music by Milton Ager. 1930 (Renewed) Warner Bros. Inc. All Rights Reserved. Used by permission. WARNER BROS. PUBLICATIONS U.S. INC., Miami, FL. 33014. 256: "Around the World" ©2002 Pearson Education, Inc. 258: "All the Way Around the World" Words and Music by Katherine Dines. Copyright ©Kiddie Korral Music. Reprinted by Permission. 260: "El Tren" (The Train) folk song from Venezuela. Canciones de Nuestra Cabaña. Reprinted by Permission. 262: "Hello!" Words and Music by Laszlo Slomovits. ©1988 ASCAP. Used by Permission. 265: "Sawatdee tuh jah" (The Hello Song) ©1998 Silver Burdett Ginn. 266: "Che che koolay" ©1995 Silver Burdett Ginn. 269: "Zudio" Arrangement ©1995 Silver Burdett Ginn. 270: "Kapulu kane" (Puili Game Song) from *Leading Young Children to Music*, 6E by Haines/Gerber ©2000. Reprinted by permission of Prentice-Hall, Inc. Upper Saddle River, NJ. 274: "El Tambor" (The Drum) from *Children's Songs of Mexico*. Copyright 1963 by Highland Music Company. Copyright assigned 1990 Alfred Publishing Co., Inc. All Rights Reserved. Used with Expressed Permission of Publisher. 277: "Diou shou juan'er" (Hide the Scarf) a Game Song from China from *Roots and Branches: A Legacy of Multicultural Music for Children* by Patricia Shehan Campbell, Ellen McCullough-Brabson, and Judith Cook Tucker. Courtesy World Music Press. Used with permission of World Music Press. English version by Pearson Education, Inc. 280: "Mon papa" (My Papa) ©2002 Pearson Education, Inc. 283: "Somebody Waiting" ©2002 Pearson Education, Inc. 285: "Haere" (Farewell) traditional Maori Song, edited and arranged by Patricia Shehan Campbell, Sue Williamson, and Pierre Perron. ©1996 Warner Bros. Publications. All Rights Reserved. Used by Permission. WARNER BROS. PUBLICATIONS U. S. INC., Miami, FL 33014. English version by Pearson Education, Inc. 286: "I'm Flying Home" Words and Music by David Eddleman. ©1991 David Eddleman. Used by Permission. All Rights Reserved. 288: "What Do Animals Need?" by the Banana Slug String Band. Reprinted by Permission. 292: "El coquí" (The Little Frog) Lyrics and Musical Arrangement Copyright ©1994, José-Luis Orozo. All Rights Reserved. Used by permission. 294: "Listen To The Water" Words and Music by Bob Schneider. ©1980 Bobally Music. All Rights Reserved. Reprinted by Permission. 296: "Chawe chidyo chem'chero" a story-song from Zimbabwe, from *African Story-Songs: Told and Sung* by Dumisani Maraire. Copyright 1969, University of Washington Press. Used by Permission. 300: "Der sad to katte" folk song. ©Used by permission MMB Music, Inc./Edition Wilhelm Hansen. 304: "Rabbit Footprints" Words and Music by David Eddleman. ©1991 David Eddleman. Used by Permission. All Rights Reserved. 305: "Rabbits" by Noah Wager. Reprinted by permission of the author. 306: "Deau-deau, ti pitit maman" (Sleep, My Little One) ©2002 Pearson Education, Inc. 308: "I Bought Me a Cat" ©1968 Silver Burdett Company. 310: "Lots of Worms" Words and Music by Patty Zeitlin. Reprinted by permission of Folklore Productions (ASCAP). 312: "Disco Worm" Words and Music by Bryan Louiselle. ©2000 Bryan Louiselle and Frog Prince Music. 318: "Don't Dump Trash" Words and Music by Jill Jarboe. Copyright ©1999 Smithsonian Folkways Recordings. SF 45048 Coco Kallis: Environmental Songs for Kids. "Don't Dump Trash" provided courtesy of Smithsonian Folkways Recordings (202) 287-3424. Reprinted by Permission. 319: "Break Free" from *Cactus Poems*, copyright ©1998 by Frank Asch, reprinted by permission of Harcourt, Inc. 320: "Every Morning When I Wake Up" words and Music by Avon Gillespie. ©1976 Belwin-Mills Publishing Corp. All Rights Reserved. Used by Permission. WARNER BROS. PUBLICATIONS U.S. INC., Miami, FL 33014. 322: "Tall Cedar Tree" Words and Music by Joseph Hillaire, as sung by Pauline Hillaire, ©1999 Pauline Hillaire. Reprinted by Permission. 323: "The Rain Song" from *Yazzie Girl* by Sharon Burch. Copyright ©1989 by Sharon Burch. Reprinted by permission of Canyon Records. 326: "To A Red Kite" from *I Thought I Heard The City* by Lilian Moore. Copyright ©1969, 1997 Lilian Moore. Used by Permission of Marian Reiner for the author. 327: "Let's Go Fly a Kite" Words and Music by Richard M. Sherman & Robert B. Sherman. ©1963 Wonderland Music Company, Inc. All Rights Reserved. Reprinted by Permission. 328: "Falling Rain" Music by April K. Kassirer, Words by Susan Marcus, from the recording *Homefree!*(©SOCAN). Used by Permission. 330: "Zip-a-Dee-Doo-Dah" Words and Music by Ray Gilbert and Allie Wribel. ©1945 Walt Disney Music Company. All Rights Reserved. Reprinted by Permission. 332: "The Rainbow" by Jean R. Thomas, from *Songs for Very Little Folks*. ©1981 Jean R. Thomas. Used with Permission. 335: "En nuestra Tierra tan linda" (On Our Beautiful Planet Earth) Lyrics and Musical Arrangement Copyright ©1997, José-Luis Orozo. From *Diez Deditos; Ten Little Fingers*. See Rights Reserved. Used by permission of the author. 336: "Tanabata-sama" (Star Festival) Japanese words by Hanayo Gondo and Ryuha Hayashi. Music by Kan-ichi Shimofusa. Copyright © 1960 by Edward B. Marks Music Company. This arrangement copyright © 2001 by Edward B. Marks Music Company. Copyright Renewed. International Copyright Secured. All Rights Reserved. Used by permission of Edward B. Marks Music Co. English version by Pearson Education, Inc. 342: "From Sea to Shining Sea" Words and Music by Gene Grier and Lowell Everson. ©1991 Heritage Music Press a division of the Lorenz Corporation International copyright secured. All Rights Reserved. Used by Permission. 346: "Sing Me a Story" Words and Music by Jill Gallina ©2000 Jill Gallina. 350: "Puff, the Magic Dragon" Words and Music by Peter Yarrow and Leonard Lipton. ©1963 Pepamar Music Corp. ©Renewed, assigned to Silver Dawn Music and Honalee Melodies. All Rights Reserved. Used by permission. WARNER BROS. PUBLICATIONS U.s. INC., Miami, FL 33014. 352: "Kibungo, Beast of the Forest" from *The Singing Sack: 28 Song-Stories from Around the World*, compiled by Helen East, A & C Black (Publishers) Limited, 1989. Reprinted by permission of the publisher. 354: "Kibungo, Beast of the Forest" from *The Singing Sack: 28 Song-Stories from Around the World*, compiled by Helen East, A & C Black (Publishers) Limited, 1989. Reprinted by permission of the publisher. English version by Pearson Education, Inc. 355: "O pião entrou" from *The Singing Sack: 28 Song-Stories from Around the World*, compiled by Helen East, A & C Black (Publishers) Limited, 1989. Reprinted by permission of the publisher. English version by Pearson Education, Inc. 357: "The Stars Streaming in the Sky" from *Wintu: The North Star* by William Brandon from The Magic World, 1991. Reprinted with the permission of Ohio University Press, Athens, Ohio. 362: "The Crocodile" ©1995 Silver Burdett Ginn. 364: "Deux cocodries" (Two Crocodiles) from *Le Hoogie Boogie: Louisiana French Music for Children* by Sharon Arms Doucet. English version by Pearson Education, Inc. Used by Permission. 366: "Jig Along Home" Words and Music by Woody Guthrie. TRO—© Copyright 1951 (Renewed) 1963 (Renewed) Ludlow Music, Inc., New York NY. Used by Permission. 370: "Look Out Below!" Words and Music by Bryan Louiselle.©2000 Bryan Louiselle and Frog Prince Music. 372: "It's a Celebration!" Words and Music by Kathering Dines. ©2000 Katherine Dines. 374: "Vamos a la fiesta" (Let's Go to the Party) Words and Music by Juanita Newland-Ulloa from *Canta Conmigo (Sing With Me)*, Bilingual Audio and Songbook Series Vol. 1-3 by Juanita Newland-Ulloa, www.juanitamusic.com. Reprinted by Permission. 376: "Skin and Bones" collected by Jean Richie. ©Jean Ritchie 1952 Geordie Music Publishing Company. Used by Permission. 377: "The Owl and the Pumpkin" from *Halloween on Parade* (GF-72). Words by Betty Barlow and Victoria Shima, Music by Betty Barlow. Copyright ©1977 Shawnee Press, Inc. Delaware Water Gap, PA 18327. International Copyright Secured. All Rights Reserved. Reprinted by Permission. 378: "Perot" (Fruit) a folksong from *Songs of Childhood*, selected and edited by Judith Eisenstein and Frieda Prensky, published 1955 by the United Synagogue Commission on Jewish Education. Used with permission of the United Synagogue Commission on Jewish Education. English version by Pearson Education, Inc. 380: "Thanksgiving Is Near" from *Holidays and Special Days*. Copyright 1998 by Alfred Publishing Co., Inc. All Rights Reserved. Used with Expressed Written Permission of Publisher. 381: "Setting the Thanksgiving Table" by X.J. Kennedy. Text copyright ©by X. J. Kennedy. First appeared in *The Kite That Braved Old Orchard Beach*, published by Margaret K. McElderry Books. Reprinted by permission of Curtis Brown, Ltd. 382: "Chanukah Is Here!" from *Songs of Childhood* selected and edited by Judith Eisenstein and Frieda Prensky, published 1955 by the United Synagogue Commission on Jewish Education. Words for this song by Judith Eisenstein, Music by Frieda Prensky. Used by Permission. 383: "Ner Li" (The Light) Words by Levin Kipnis and Music by Mifalei Tarbuth. ©Music by Mifalei Tarbuth Vekhinukh, Acum, Israel, Lyrics by the author, Acum, Israel. Used by permission of Acum Ltd. English version by Silver Burdett Ginn. 384: "O laufet, ihr Hirten" (Come Running, You Shepherds) from *The International Book of Christmas Carols* by Ehret/Evans, ©1964. Reprinted by permission of Prentice-Hall, Inc., Upper Saddle River, NJ. 385: "It's Santa Again" from *Come Join In*. Copyright 1996 by Alfred Publishing Co., Inc. All Rights Reserved. Used with Expressed Written Permission of Publisher. 386: "Christmas Don't Be Late" (The Chipmunk Song) from *1,000 Jumbo—The Children's Song Book* by Charles Hansen Distributor, Educational Sheet Music and Books, 1860 Broadway, New York, NY. ©1958 by Monarch Music Corp., Los Angeles, CA. 391: "Mister Snow Rap" ©2000 Linda Walsh. 392: "Kwanzaa Carol" Words and Music by Reggie Royal. ©1999 Reijiro Music. Reprinted by Permission. 394: "A Kid Like Me" Words and Music by Cathy Fink and Marcy Marxer, from *Nobody Else Like Me*, by Cathy Fink and Marcy Marxer. ©1993, 2 Spoons Music (ASCAP). Rounder Kids CD 8021. Used with Permission. 396: "Free at Last" Arrangement ©1995 Silver Burdett Ginn. 397: "When I Grow Up" by Jack Prelutsky, from *A Pizza the Size of the Sun*. Text copyright © 1996 by Jack Prelutsky. Used by permission of HarperCollins Publishers. 398: "Valentines" by Burt Szabo. Copyright 1999 by Choral Concepts. Reprinted by permission of Burt Szabo. 400: "L'inverno è passato" (Winter Is Over) ©2002 Pearson Education, Inc. 401: "Haru ga kita" (Springtime Has Come) Words and Music by Okano Teiichi and Patty Zeitlin. Reprinted by permission of Folklore Productions. 402: "America, I Hear You Singing" Words and Music by Barberi Paull. ©1991 by Barberi Paull. Reprinted by Permission. The editors of Scott Foresman have made every attempt to verify the source of "Mariposita" (Little Butterfly)(p. 156), "Cat's Menu" (p. 301), but were unable to do so. The editors of Scott Foresman have made every effort to locate all copyright holders of material used in this book. If any errors or omissions have occurred, corrections will be made.

433

Index of Songs

A-Tisket, A-Tasket, p. 238 CD 8–24
Abiyoyo, p. 108 CD 4–25
Achshav (Awake! Awake!), p. 64 CD 3–1
Adana ya gidelim (Let's Go to Adana), p. 142
    CD 5–32
All Around the Buttercup, p. 170 CD 6–26
All the Way Around the World, p. 258 CD 9–19
Allá en la fuente (There at the Spring), p. 92
    CD 3–48
Amarillo Armadillo, p. 82 CD 3–33
America, p. 403 CD 15–11
America, I Hear You Singing, p. 402 CD 15–9
Are You Sleeping? *(Frère Jacques)*, p. 125 CD 5–2
Awake! Awake! *(Achshav)*, p. 64 CD 3–2
Ayelivi, p. 70 CD 3–9

Banana, p. 114 CD 4–32
Banjo Sam, p. 314 CD 11–22
Bob-a-Needle, p. 232 CD 8–19
Boogie Chant and Dance (speech piece), p. 78
    CD 3–22
Boysie, p. 195 CD 7–25
But the Cat Came Back, p. 190 CD 7–16

Caballito blanco (Little White Pony), p. 193 CD 7–18
Chanukah Is Here! p. 382 CD 14–15
Chawe chidyo chem'chero p. 297 CD 11–2
Che che koolay, p. 266 CD 9–32
Cheki, morena (Shake It!), p. 180 CD 7–1
Chicka Hanka, p. 211 CD 8–1
"Chirimbolo" Game, The *(El juego chirimbolo)*, p. 54
    CD 2–28
Christmas, Don't Be Late, p. 386 CD 14–27
Chuhwuht, p. 356 CD 13–12
Ciranda (A Ring of Roses), p. 272 CD 10–1
Clouds of Gray, p. 56 CD 2–32
Come Running, You Shepherds *(O laufet, ihr Hirten)*,
    p. 384 CD 14–22
Cookie, p. 172 CD 6–31
Crawfish! p. 86 CD 3–41
Crocodile, The, p. 362 CD 13–19

Deau-deau, ti pitit maman (Sleep, My Little One)
    p. 306 CD 11–13
Der sad to katte (Two Cats), p. 300 CD 11–5
Deux cocodries (Two Crocodiles), p. 364 CD 13–21
Dinah, p. 120 CD 4–39
Dinosaur Dance, The, p. 168 CD 6–24
Diou shou juan'er (Hide the Scarf), p. 277 CD 10–12
Don't Dump Trash, p. 318 CD 11–26
Down, Down, Baby, p. 32 CD 1–41
Down the Ohio, p. 60 CD 2–42
Drum, The *(El tambor)*, p. 274 CD 10–8
Duck Dance, p. 249 CD 9–9

Ein Männlein steht im Walde (A Little Man in the
    Woods), p. 90 CD 3–43
El coquí (The Little Frog), p. 292 CD 10–36
El florón (The Flower), p. 246 CD 9–1
El juego chirimbolo (The "Chirimbolo" Game), p. 54
    CD 2–27
El tambor (The Drum), p. 274 CD 10–7
El tren (The Train), p. 260 CD 9–21
Elephant, An (Un elefante), p. 160 CD 6–13
En nuestra Tierra tan linda, p. 335 CD 12–9
Ev'ry Kind of Music, p. 226 CD 8–14
Every Morning When I Wake Up, p. 320 CD 11–28

Falling Rain, p. 328 CD 12–1
Farewell *(Haere)*, p. 285 CD 10–28
Farmer's Dairy Key, The, p. 182 CD 7–6
Flower, The *(El florón)*, p. 246 CD 9–2
Four in a Boat, p. 46 CD 2–13
Free at Last, p. 396 CD 14–40
Frère Jacques (Are You Sleeping?), p. 125 CD 5–1
Frog in the Millpond, p. 44 CD 2–8
From Sea to Shining Sea, p. 342 CD 12–19
Fruit *(Perot)*, p. 378 CD 14–10

Glad to Have a Friend Like You, p. 228 CD 8–16
Go Around the Corn, Sally, p. 12 CD 1–8
Gonna Have a Good Time, p. 4 CD 1–1
Good Mornin', Blues, p. 52 CD 2–24
Great Big House, p. 204 CD 7–42

and Speech Pieces

Ha'kyo jong (School Bell Sounding), p. 135
CD 5–22

Haere (Farewell), p. 285 CD 10–27

Happy Feet, p. 252 CD 9–15

Haru ga kita (Springtime Has Come), p. 401
CD 15–5

Heigh-Ho, p. 7 CD 1–3

Hello! p. 262 CD 9–25

Hello Song, The *(Sawatdee tuh jah)*, p. 265
CD 9–29

Hide the Scarf *(Diou shou juan'er)*, p. 277 CD 10–13

Home from School *(Hui jia qù)*, p. 158
CD 6–6

How Many Miles to Babylon? p. 128
CD 5–10

Hui jia qù (Home from School), p. 158 CD 6–5

I Bought Me a Cat, p. 308 CD 11–17

I Fed My Horse, p. 94 CD 4–1

I Got Shoes, p. 242 CD 8–30

I See the Moon, p. 58 CD 2–37

I See with My Hands, p. 148 CD 5–47

I'm Flying Home, p. 286 CD 10–31

Ise oluwa, p. 102 CD 4–17

It's a Celebration! p. 372 CD 13–30

It's Santa—Again! p. 385 CD 14–25

Ja-Da, p. 188 CD 7–13

Jelly in a Dish (speech piece), p. 83 CD 3–38

Jig Along Home, p. 366 CD 13–25

Jingle Bells, p. 388 CD 14–30

Kapulu kane (Puili Game Song), p. 270
CD 9–37

Kibungo, p. 354 CD 13–2

Kid Like Me, A, p. 394 CD 14–38

Kou ri lengay (The Strength of the Lion), p. 217
CD 8–7

Kwanzaa Carol, A, p. 392 CD 14–36

L'inverno è passato (Winter Is Over), p. 400
CD 15–1

La mar estaba serena (The Sea is Calm), p. 345
CD 12–21

La tormenta tropical (The Tropical Storm), p. 116
CD 4–34

Leatherwing Bat, p. 303 CD 11–9

Let's Go Fly a Kite, p. 327 CD 11–36

Let's Go to Adana *(Adana ya gidelim)*,
p. 142 CD 5–33

Let's Go to the Party *(Vamos a la fiesta)*,
p. 374 CD 14–2

Light, The *(Ner li)*, p. 383 CD 14–18

Listen to the Water, p. 294 CD 10–40

Little Bird, A *(Un pajarito)*, p. 16 CD 1–21

Little Butterfly *(Mariposita)*, p. 156 CD 6–2

Little Frog, The *(El coquí)*, p. 292 CD 10–37

Little Man in the Woods, A *(Ein Männlein steht im
Walde)*, p. 90 CD 3–44

Little White Pony *(Caballito blanco)*, p. 193
CD 7–19

Lone Star Trail, p. 21 CD 1–26

Look Out Below! p. 370 CD 13–28

Lots of Worms, p. 310 CD 11–19

Lucy Locket, p. 27 CD 1–32

Mariposita (Little Butterfly), p. 156 CD 6–1

Michael, Row the Boat Ashore, p. 18 CD 1–24

Miss Mary Mack, p. 42 CD 2–4

Mississippi River Chant (speech piece), p. 132
CD 5–20

Mister Snow Rap (speech piece), p. 391 CD 14–34

Mon papa (My Papa), p. 280 CD 10–17

Music's in Me, The, p. 40 CD 2–2

My Father's House, p. 25 CD 1–29

My Foot's In My Stirrup, p. 234 CD 8–21

My Papa *(Mon papa)*, p. 280 CD 10–18

Naranja dulce (Sweet Orange), p. 96 CD 4–3

Ner li (The Light), p. 383 CD 14–17

O laufet, ihr Hirten (Come Running, You
Shepherds), p. 384 CD 14–21

O pião entrou (The Top Joined the Circle), p. 355
CD 13–6

Oh, Watch the Stars, p. 144 CD 5–38

Old Brass Wagon, p. 122 CD 4–44

One, Two, Three *(Un, deux, trois)*, p. 198 CD 7–32

Owl and the Pumpkin, The, p. 377 CD 14–7

Song Index

Party Tonight! p. 152 CD 5–50
Perot (Fruit), p. 378 CD 14–9
Piñon, pirulín, p. 174 CD 6–33
Pizza, Pizza, Daddy-o, p. 28 CD 1–36
Plant Four Seeds, p. 130 CD 5–17
Puff, the Magic Dragon, p. 350 CD 12–28

R

Rabbit Footprints, p. 304 CD 11–11
Ragtime Cowboy Joe, p. 250 CD 9–12
Rainbow, The, p. 332 CD 12–6
Riddle Ree (speech piece), p. 34 CD 1–43
Ring of Roses, A *(Ciranda)*, p. 272 CD 10–2
Rocky Mountain, p. 98 CD 4–7
Rosie, Darling Rosie, p. 215 CD 8–5

Same Train, p. 164 CD 6–20
Sawatdee tuh jah (The Hello Song), p. 265 CD 9–28
School Bell Sounding *(Ha'kyo jong)*, p. 135 CD 5–23
Sea is Calm, The *(La mar estaba serena)*, p. 345
  CD 12–22
Sea Shell, p. 100 CD 4–12
See-Saw Sacradown, p. 208 CD 7–49
Shake It! *(Cheki, morena)*, p. 180 CD 7–2
Shake Them 'Simmons Down, p. 244 CD 8–32
She'll Be Comin' 'Round the Mountain, p. 358
  CD 13–15
Shoo, Fly, p. 200 CD 7-38
Silver Moon Boat *(Xiao yin chuan)*, p. 14 CD 1–14
Sing a Rainbow, p. 166 CD 6–22
Sing Me a Story, p. 346 CD 12–25
Skin and Bones, p. 376 CD 14–5
Sleep, Baby, Sleep, p. 197 CD 7–27
Sleep, My Little One *(Deau-deau, ti pitit maman)*,
  p. 306 CD 11–14
Somebody Waiting, p. 283 CD 10–23
Song of the Eagle, p. 248 CD 9–6
Song That's Just for You, A, p. 126 CD 5–8
Springtime Has Come *(Haru ga kita)*, p. 401
  CD 15–6
Star Festival *(Tanabata-sama)*, p. 336 CD 12–13
Step in Time, p. 74 CD 3–19
Strength of the Lion, The (Kou ri lengay), p. 217
  CD 8–7
Sweet Orange *(Naranja dulce)*, p. 96 CD 4–4

Tall Cedar Tree, p. 322 CD 11–30
Tanabata-sama (Star Festival), p. 336 CD 12–12
Thanksgiving Is Near, p. 380 CD 14–13
There at the Spring *(Allá en la fuente)*, p. 92
  CD 3–49
Tideo, p. 80 CD 3–26
Time to Sing, p. 8 CD 1–5
Top Joined the Circle, The *(O pião entrou)*, p. 355
  CD 13–7
Train, The *(El tren)*, p. 260 CD 9–22
Tree in the Wood, The, p. 360 CD 13–17
Tropical Storm, The *(La tormenta tropical)*, p. 116
  CD 4–35
Trouble Is a Mountain, p. 202 CD 7–40
Two Cats *(Der sad to katte)*, p. 300 CD 11–6
Two Crocodiles *(Deux cocodries)*, p. 364 CD 13–22
Two Little Sausages (speech piece), p. 79 CD 3–24

Un, deux, trois (One, Two, Three), p. 198 CD 7-31
Un elefante (An Elephant), p. 160 CD 6–12
Un pajarito (A Little Bird), p. 16 CD 1–20

Valentines, p. 398 CD 14–42
Vamos a la fiesta (Let's Go to the Party), p. 374
  CD 14–1

Waiting for the Traffic Light, p. 107 CD 4–23
Way Down in the Schoolyard, p. 50 CD 2–21
We're All Gonna Shine Tonight, p. 240 CD 8–27
What Do Animals Need? p. 288 CD 10–34
When the Saints Go Marching In, p. 178 CD 6–41
Who Has Seen the Wind? p. 324 CD 11–33
Winter Is Over *(L'inverno è passato)*, p. 400 CD 15–2

Xiao yin chuan (Silver Moon Boat), p. 14 CD 1–13

Yankee Doodle, p. 405 CD 15–13

Zip-a-Dee-Doo-Dah, p. 330 CD 12–4
Zudio, p. 269 CD 9–35